Smoo004237
27-3-01
£18.99
K4
(Ric)

Using NVivo in
Qualitative Research

0761965246

Using NVivo in Qualitative Research

Lyn Richards

SAGE Publications

London • Thousand Oaks • New Delhi

SAGE Publications Ltd.
6 Bonhill Street
London EC2A 4PU

SAGE Publications Inc.
2455 Teller Road
Thousand Oaks, California 91320

SAGE Publications India Pvt Ltd.
32, M-Block Market
Greater Kailash - I
New Delhi 110 048

Trademarks

Copyright © Qualitative Solutions and Research Pty. Ltd. Melbourne, Australia. 1999 (ACN 006 357 213). All rights reserved.

NVivo, NUD*IST, NUD*IST Vivo, NUDIST, NUDIST Vivo and the NVivo logo are trademarks or registered trademarks of Qualitative Solutions and Research Pty. Ltd. Microsoft Windows, Windows NT, Windows 95, Microsoft Word, Wordpad, Excel are trademarks or registered trademarks of Microsoft Corporation. SPSS is a registered trademark of SPSS Inc. GB-STAT is a trademark of Dynamic Microsystems Inc. Decision Explorer is a trademark of Banxia Software. Wordperfect is a registered trademark of Corel Corporation.

British Library Cataloguing in Publication data

A catalogue record for this book is available from the British Library

ISBN   0-7619-6524-6
ISBN (pbk)   0-7619-6525-4

Library of Congress catalog card available

Typeset by Kirstie Taylor
Printed in Great Britain by The Alden Press, Oxford

Contents

Chapter 4: Nodes 53

Preface

This is a book about doing qualitative research with a particular software package, QSR NUD*IST Vivo (NVivo). QSR provides two books with NVivo, and this one is about the research process, not about how to do particular tasks with the software. Our aim is that it works, not as a manual works, to instruct in the mechanics of software use, but as a methods text, exploring techniques and their analytical results. For how-to advice, go to the *QSR NUD*IST Vivo: Reference Guide*, and to the on-line Help, which describe the NVivo commands, dialogs and functions in detail.

In a decade of software development QSR has developed new ways of teaching and assisting researchers using its software, and this book is a result of their feedback. Please let us know how it works for you. Thousands of users in over forty countries have contributed indirectly to the development of supporting materials for the NUD*IST software, by expressing their needs and telling us what helped and what didn't. Hundreds who are active on the QSR-Forum contributed ideas and challenges, accounts of getting stuck and getting clear, ways of explaining and new ways of seeing through research puzzles and forming research strategies. The book draws also on what we have learned from working with, training and listening to colleague researchers around the world who teach and assist researchers using QSR's software. Some are well known figures, whose services are listed on the website, some unsung helpers who assist others. We thank them all, and invite more feedback!

The book, like the software, is a team product, a result of five years' work by the software development team at Qualitative Solutions and Research. It has been helped by team discussions, debates over nomenclature, fights over functions, and indirectly by everyone at QSR. It had direct contributions from Tom Richards, Don Fraser and Ted Barrington, and was edited and designed by Kirstie Taylor.

Lyn Richards,

September, 1999.

Chapter 1: About this book

Why a book about doing qualitative research with a particular software package? In the past decade, qualitative computing has become widely accepted, even required, and packages have become far more sophisticated. However, ways of learning software skills have progressed more slowly. As software packages have grown from simple code and retrieve systems to much more complex toolkits supporting a very wide range of methods and methodologies, materials exploring and explaining these tools have lagged behind.

The few studies of researchers using such packages have shown a wide range of experiences, including very negative ones, especially for novice researchers thrown into computing and qualitative methods simultaneously. Teachers and researchers have begun to demand full documentation, teaching and self-teaching materials, and discussions not only of how to work the software but also of issues of research design and analysis, methodological options and software processes. Such materials are also needed by readers and reviewers of research whose different task is to evaluate the processes by which conclusions are drawn.

The software explored in this book is widely regarded as offering a new stage in software development. QSR NUD*IST Vivo (NVivo) supports new project structures and new research processes. Together, these provide very new choices for management and analysis of data. The software combines the coding of rich data with familiar ways of editing and revising rich text, so is much easier to introduce to students than previous programs which reduced rich data to plain and fairly static text.

The software can be learned during research rather than in prolonged preparatory training phases. But such learning by doing requires that researchers have a prior overview, a map of the toolkit and its uses. This book provides that map.

Software accompanies the book. The CD carries a version of NVivo that has all the functionality of the full software, except that it does not save changes to a project. It can be used in either of two modes. In Tutorial mode, it will run any of five different tutorial projects with step-by-step help text. The tutorials offer different sorts of data, from different settings, giving a choice of skills to be learned. In Viewer mode, any project can be viewed and explored, but changes not saved. Load the CD and it will walk you through to the choice appropriate for your purposes.

Who can use this book?

Understanding the software: for supervisors, colleagues, research clients

This book can be read alone if you want to know about the potential of software for qualitative research, or if you want to understand the software being used by colleagues or students. It is intended to assist not only researchers who help or supervise users, but those who want to know what qualitative software can offer research, and those who review or use the results of research, and wish to understand the supporting software.

Use the software in Viewer mode, following the instructions to open any project and explore it without changing it. In this way NVivo allows qualitative projects to be viewed and reviewed by supervisors, research participants or clients. This book will help such recipients of projects to understand and access them, to evaluate and critique the processes by which data can be managed and explored, and assess analyses conducted in NVivo.

Introductory level learning: for students, self-teaching researchers, explorers

This book can be used in conjunction with any of the tutorials on the CD. The tutorials offer a choice of data type and disciplinary area, for students learning about qualitative computing, and for researchers trying out the software or taking the first steps to learn it.

If you do not have the full software, use this book to help you to understand what it can do, and use the tutorial's help texts to try doing it. (These are also available with the full software). Supplement your learning with the very detailed Help online in the demonstration or full version of the software. These are, of course, not substitutes for the *Reference Manual* that comes with the full software, but they will suffice to let you try out the software, get a feel for the way you can work using it, and get started.

The design of NVivo integrates a very wide range of tools in a symmetrical and quite simple structure. This integration means that you can start a project and get going in NVivo as you learn it, so not all techniques need to be learned up front. This book will provide background to what you learn, and an overview to help you assess this experience for your own research purposes.

Teachers can create their own projects, with data relevant to their classes, and students can learn on that data with the software provided on the CD in the back of this book. Projects will not save for future devlopment, but all the tools can be tried, discussed and learnt.

Commencing research with NVivo: users and research colleagues

If you have the full QSR NUD*IST Vivo (NVivo) software, this book accompanied the software, along with the detailed *Reference Manual*. The two are structured symmetrically. Except for the first and last chapters, the topics are covered in the same order, and the chapter numbers match in both.

If you are teaching yourself with the full software, move between this book and the *Reference Manual* at each stage. They are designed together to introduce you to each of the data structures and research processes the software supports, and to research design and analysis strategies you may use as you develop your own project. Team members and colleagues can use the no-save tutorial version of the software to achieve familiarity with the program.

Qualitative research and NVivo

Qualitative research is varied, and different qualitative methodologies have very different goals. This book will not tell you how to locate your research in the range of methodologies, but when you do so, it will help you to find the appropriate tools in the software.

Qualitative researchers rarely work with a fixed body of previously collected data. You are likely to have changing and growing rich records built up from observations, interviews, document analysis, literature reviews and other research media. Their sources vary (e.g., field notes, transcripts, scanned documents) and they come in many forms (such as text, photographs, tapes, films). NVivo provides a range of tools for handling rich data records and information about them for browsing and enriching text, coding it visually or at categories, annotating and gaining accessed data records accurately and swiftly.

Qualitative research usually also treats as *data* the records of ideas about these research events and reflections on them. NVivo has tools for recording and linking ideas in many ways, and for searching and exploring the patterns of data and ideas. It is designed to remove rigid divisions between "data" and "interpretation" – if this is what the researcher wishes. It offers many ways of connecting the parts of a project, integrating reflection and recorded data.

Qualitative research usually requires management of complexity. As you link, code, shape and model data, the software helps you to manage and synthesize your ideas. It offers a range of tools for pursuing new understandings and theories about the data and for constructing and testing answers to research questions.

What this book does not do

This book describes what can be done, and how to use what you can do with the tools provided by NVivo. It advises on research strategies and choices. It aims to help researchers maximize the usefulness of the tools provided by the software, and reflect on the methodological implications and possibilities of what they can do with it. It is about what you might be trying to do and what the software offers, rather than about either the methodological assumptions behind what you are doing, or the particular techniques for doing it.

It is not a qualitative methods text, nor does it review software tools for handling qualitative data. It assumes a reader who knows at least broadly what they are trying to do, and wants to know how to do it in NVivo.

If you are new to qualitative research, you are advised to explore the literature on qualitative methods, and particularly to locate your research project within the very wide choice of ways of handling and interpreting data. Each researcher will choose from and use these tools differently, depending on their research methods and goals. This book does not describe or evaluate different qualitative methods, or teach how to use them. Instead, it provides the overview of the toolkit with attention to the range of uses of each tool, so you can make such choices thoughtfully, and approach your project with an understanding of the ways the software can assist what you are wanting to do. For wider reading on qualitative methods, and links to other reading sources, visit the QSR website: www.qsr.com.au.

This book does not include instructions on using the software. For how to do it, the detailed instructions about menu items and mouse clicks, Help texts are provided in the software, brief do-it-yourself texts are provided with the tutorials, and full instructions are in the *Reference Manual*.

Using this book

This book is organized to be rapidly consulted or to be read sequentially, like a methods book.

Chapter 2 introduces NVivo, explaining how the software tools are integrated in a Project.

Chapters 3-5 introduce the three systems with which a researcher builds up a project, Documents, Nodes, and Attributes.

Each of these chapters starts with an Overview, and explains the choices available, offering advice for designing, starting and managing this part of your project. Use the directions in parentheses to go back to discussions of functions and techniques you may otherwise overlook. These are italicized throughout the book, for example: *(See Chapter 3: Documents)*.

The remaining chapters cover the processes supported by combinations of these building blocks: Linking data, Coding at nodes, Shaping data –Sets and Trees, Modeling and Searching. The concluding chapter is an overview of the different ways these tools support connecting and analyzing, and the ways that supervisors, recipients or team members can assess and contribute to research – Getting it Together.

Parts of a Project		Processes of a Project	
Ch3	Documents - data, reflections, memos - rich text	**Ch6**	Linking
Ch4	Nodes - Ideas, categories, concepts, people, things - flexibly managed.	**Ch7**	Coding
Ch5	Attributes - of documents or nodes: values given, changed, viewed	**Ch8**	Sets
		Ch9	Modeling
Parts and processes of a project - and the central chapters of this book are the *Reference Manual.*		**Ch10**	Searching

Many researchers using the software will be familiar with at least some of these processes, and most will not want to use all of them. The book is designed to be read sequentially for a complete overview, or to be used by skimming or dipping for access to particular techniques. Skimmers and dippers should however be aware that every aspect of the software, including those found also in the architecture of its partner software package, NUD*IST4, is new.

Finally, a note for users of previous qualitative software packages. The assumption of familiarity with software processes can lead you to overlook tools that are new, or processes newly available. This is particularly true of NVivo, which departs from previous software because it is designed to free researchers from the necessity to think by coding. As Chapter 3 shows, thinking can be recorded using rich text editing of data documents and memos. As Chapter 4 shows, thinking can be located at nodes without coding. The following chapters suggest ways of using entirely new techniques for linking data and shaping them in sets, then ways of combining these with the new coding processes in NVivo and the new modeling and searching facilities. The final chapter explores the new ways for getting your data and your ideas together.

NVivo is an entirely new partner product and optional upgrade to the QSR NUD*IST software whose current version, NUD*IST revision 4, (nicknamed N4) is the leading software for qualitative analysis. Users of N4 upgrading to NVivo can take a project directly into the new software. Hence there are tips for N4 users identified in each chapter. For systematic comparison of the two products, visit QSR's website. (The tutorial entitled "Import NUDIST" carries simple instructions for importing a project from N4.)

Chapter 2: A Project in NVivo

To do research with NVivo, you create a project to hold the information, data, observations, ideas and most importantly the connections between them relevant to your research task. This chapter summarizes how a project is constructed, showing how researchers can use the tools appropriate to their methods for organizing, linking, questioning and synthesizing.

Overview

- To work with data in NVivo, you create a project that holds the data and the ideas about it and links between them;

- The structure of any project is simple and symmetrical. The research processes supported can be as simple or complex as you wish;

- There can be three systems for managing data in any project: documents, nodes and attributes;

- The processes of a project bring these systems together in giving values to attributes, linking, coding and shaping in sets the documents and nodes;

- All of these parts of a project can be represented in "live" models;

- Searches of text or coding are integrated, and the user can specify the scope for any search, in terms of documents, nodes or attribute values;

- Any number of projects can be created. A project can be accessed and altered by any number of team members, but only by one at any given time.

You choose between a typical, single-user project, or a custom setup in which you can give different access to different team members. The project is created in the folder you specify.

Go to the *Reference Manual*, Chapter 2, for instructions on using the software to create a project and set controls for multi-access projects, and how to save and back up a project.

Getting started

To start the software, follow directions on the tutorial disk, or in the *Reference Manual*. When you call NVivo, a window appears with the Launch Pad below the NVivo menu bar. It offers the choices of opening a new or existing project or a tutorial project.

A Project Pad appears whichever project you open. Its tabs and buttons map the structure of a project in NVivo and give access to the most common activities. If you do not wish the Project Pad to stay on the screen you can reduce it to its menu bar - go to Windows on the menubar and click on Project Pad. If you leave it open you can work from it for quick access to each part of your project. You may choose to close it, but first study the symmetry of the parts and processes it maps. In any project in NVivo, the researcher can create and explore documents and nodes, as data is browsed, linked and coded. Documents and nodes can be given the values of attributes, to store information about them. Documents and nodes can be managed in sets. And all of these can be involved in modeling and searching.

> *Don't assume the Pad is only for beginners. It is designed not only to offer a map of an NVivo project for newcomers, but also to act as research assistant for more confident users, offering immediate access to each of the main NVivo windows. From this small window you can access all major functions.*

NVivo's Parts and Processes

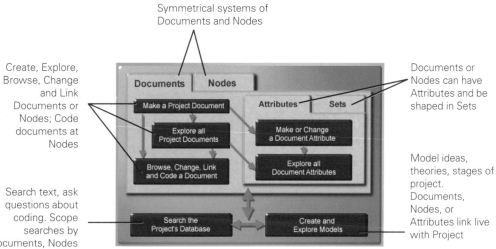

As the Pad shows, a project has a database of documents and nodes, which can be explored, browsed, linked and coded. Documents and nodes can be handled by storing attributes or grouping in Sets. The analysis tools provide for Searching and Modeling.

The types of data in a project

There can be three systems for managing data in any Project. Each of these parts of your project is clearly identified by icons in the software.

Documents

Documents in NVivo are plain or rich text records that can be made compound if you embed in them links to picture, video, audio, spreadsheet, database, or other data items that your computer can handle.

You can import documents, from a word processor, into your project in rich text (or ordinary plain text) computer files. Once in the project you can still edit them and keep "writing them up" in rich text.

You can create your documents inside your NVivo project if you wish, and add to them throughout the lifetime of your project.

You can create Proxy documents inside your project to represent data you don't wish to include directly. Examples include books or other paper documents, data on audio or video tape, huge computer files you don't want to include in their entirety or data you only wish to have summaries of in your project.

Nodes

A Node is the container in NVivo for categories and coding. Nodes can represent any categories - concepts, people, abstract ideas, places and any other things that matter to your project. Nodes can be kept without organization as Free Nodes, or organized hierarchically, if you wish, in Trees.

Because qualitative researchers normally move between documents and ideas about them, the document and node systems are symmetrical in NVivo. You can explore and browse both, and you move between the systems by coding and linking. When you code any part of a document at a node, you place their references to passages of text. You can then browse all the data coded there, rethink, recode, and ask questions about the category in searches.

Attributes of Documents and Nodes

Both documents and nodes can have attributes whose values can represent any property you like. Thus you can store information about any document (e.g. gender=female or date=1999) or about the object, person or concept a node represents. Attributes can be used in searches.

You can create and change the attributes, and store any amount of information about a document or a node by specifying the values of its attributes. For example, if your documents were fieldnotes, you might create an attribute "Location" and another "Visit date". Give each document the appropriate value and you can now ask for all the material on a topic from a particular rural location, or from before the drought broke. If you have case studies of individuals throughout the data documents, each can be given a node coding everything about that case. The node might have an attribute "gender" with values "female" and "male"; now you can ask for everything about a woman if it was in fieldnotes from a rural area.

Each of these types of data: documents, nodes, and their attributes, are managed in an Explorer window.

The processes of a project

The parts of a project come together as you:

- Characterize your documents and nodes by giving them values for the attributes you have set up;

- Create DataLinks (DataBites, DocLinks and NodeLinks) connecting related documents and nodes to each other and to other data;

- Code documents or any part of them at nodes to record where the topic or concept represented by the node, occurs in the text;

- Shape the project by managing documents or nodes in Sets, to explore or ask questions;

- Make and change visual graphical Models of your ideas or project processes;

- Search text or coding, using an armory of special-purpose searches integrated in one Search tool, to answer questions and build theories.

These processes are independent but integrated.

Working in NVivo

All the parts and processes discussed above are integrated, with symmetrically organized tools to handle them.

Explorers

Each of a project's areas is viewed and investigated through an Explorer window that contains information about the whole area, (for example about all documents) and gives access to other tools that work on that area.

◆ The Document Explorer and Node Explorer provide access to all documents and nodes respectively, allowing you to create more of them and compare, investigate and access them;

◆ Two Attribute Explorers perform the same function for document and node attributes. In them you can create, delete, view, add to or change attributes and their values for different documents and nodes;

◆ The Modeler allows you to create and edit a graphical representation of your data and ideas. You can place in it new ideas or project documents, nodes or attributes and link and group them visually. Further you can create and change styles of representation, set up layers and shapes and compare the model with any number of other models. The Model Explorer lists and shows the items in all the graphical models created.

Browsers

If you ask to browse a document or a node, you are taken to a Document Browser or Node Browser. Browsers, unlike Explorers, show you the contents of one single data item, such as one document. In Document and Node Browsers, you see the text of the chosen document or node as rich text.

You can code in either browser, linking the text you select to a node on this topic. In the Document Browser you can also edit the text of the document in rich text format, and without disturbing any coding you have done.

Different goals, different processes: how the parts combine

Different researchers with different purposes will use and combine all the above-mentioned tools and parts of a project differently, in interlocking processes of data management and analysis:

A quick, descriptive project might take minutes to set up (for example, a pilot project using focus group transcripts to explore an issue). It might start with only a few documents, (or only one Project Document holding a transcript or

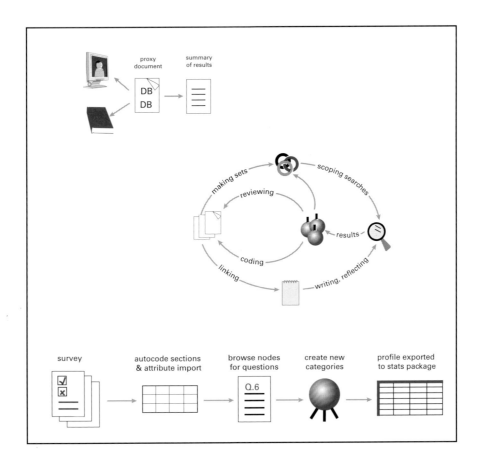

summary of the transcripts). The group moderator's notes are coded by the automatic Section Coder at nodes representing the main questions asked. The researcher might then use rich text editing for Visual Coding, storing in annotations the growing ideas about themes in the answers to each question. Patterns in the data can be reported with neat matrix summaries or rich text output (perhaps with video clips from the group discussion) for immediate display.

A long-term, detailed project would involve very different processes. Such a project might use a grounded theory or other theory-constructing methodology with rich text records of data such as in-depth interviews and field notes. This project might start with research design documents linked to annotations, audio tape segments, literature reviews and rich text memos recording growing understanding of the data. Documents would grow in complexity with links to other documents and nodes. Coding would create early categories stored in Free Nodes and refined by coding-on from the retrieved material to new nodes. Ideas would be sketched in models whose layers represent different ways of looking at the data. As analysis proceeded, nodes would be shaped in Trees to express catalogues of like categories, or filtered in Sets to give access to different analysis areas and scope searches. Text and coding search explores occurrences of core themes.

A sample survey project (with open ended questions) might have many documents. Attribute values record information about respondents. Answers to questions are coded automatically using NVivo's "Section Coding" processes. Researchers would create new nodes as they post-code, creating coding categories from the text of answers. Using those nodes, they might test for patterns of responses and display them in a live matrix. Graphical models illustrate the patterns in reports.

The following tables offer an overview:

NVivo at a glance:

ORGANIZING PROCESSES	Documents	Nodes
Selecting data types for different purposes	Text can be imported and edited (or written) in rich text format, (including italics, font, color etc) with up to nine levels of Sections. Data sources external to the project can be represented in proxy documents: including text, pictures, audio or video clips.	Nodes represent ideas, things, people, concepts, categories for thinking about data: Use Free Nodes for unorganized ideas; Tree Nodes to organize your nodes into a hierarchical thesaurus-like system; Case Nodes manage all data on cases.
Describing the data	Use document and node descriptions to store information about context etc, define categories, shape ideas.	
Changing data and ideas	Browse text in the Document Browser. Edit freely (full rich text edit capacity) to add, delete text, annotate or underline, color etc for impact, change heading level and sections. Code the document in the Browser; code and edit concurrently. Use various techniques to show what nodes code the text in the Browser.	Browse what the Node codes in the Node Browser. Jump to the relevant document to edit it. Change the context in which you view the coding. Code the text in the Browser. Use various techniques to show what other nodes code the text in the Browser.

ORGANIZING PROCESSES	Documents	Nodes
Viewing and managing	Document Explorer shows documents with information and outline of document in sections; jump to Browse document as a whole or go straight to selected section.	Node Explorer shows all nodes by type, gives information including coding status and properties. Drag and drop to reorganize. Explore and move around the categories, changing the index system as ideas form and merge (move with drag&drop, delete, cut, copy, paste, merge coding).
Grouping and accessing	Documents or nodes can be put in any number of Sets, and Sets are integrated in all processes - code with a Set, ask questions about a Set, filter a Set by their coding or attributes.	
Storing and using information; Attributes	Create, edit and investigate any number of attributes of documents or nodes, with any number of Values: use these to store any amount of information about the document, the node, or what they represent (people, sites, cases etc.). Rapidly import attributes and values, from spreadsheets or statistical packages. Explore and alter attributes and values in a flexible on-screen display.	

NVivo provides several entirely new "hyperlinks" - ways of linking documents to external files, annotations, other documents or ideas.

LINKING PROCESSES	Documents	Nodes
Linking to annotations or any other multimedia files	Select text and create DataBites, which link to textual Annotations (to comment on the selected text), or to any external file including pictures, audio or video clips. Use DataBites to illustrate or enrich the data, making compound documents with dynamic, multimedia records of events, project planning, etc.	Code the text including any DataBites in it - and they can be accessed from text coded at the node.
Linking to documents, including rich text memos	Link documents to other documents or nodes. Use a DocLink to link any document(s) from a node, from any place in text of a document, from a node.	

LINKING PROCESSES	*Documents*	*Nodes*
Memos	Any document can be classed a Memo. Memos do not have to be linked to other documents or nodes. Any document or node or any text can have any number of memos. Memos are full status documents (rich text, codable, linkable).	
Linking to Nodes	Use a NodeLink to link a document, any place in its text or any node to a node. Use the NodeLink to take you to all the data on a topic or to remind you of related categories.	
Linking to a particular passage or quotation	Use a NodeLink to make an Extract node, coding at it just the text you want to jump to. It leads you from a document or a node to a relevant document passage or passages. This functions like a citation footnote.	

NVivo supports coding of documents at categories (by many methods) and exploring rethinking and revising coded material.

CODING PROCESSES	**Documents**	**Nodes**
Coding documents	Code text in documents. Use rich text editing for Visual Coding (font, color etc to show emphasis or meaning). Code by placing references to the text at a node using the Document Browser or Node Browser.	Make nodes for your coding categories. Create them as Free Nodes or Tree Nodes or Case Nodes as appropriate.
Choosing coding method:	Code by any of several methods in either the Document or the Node Browser. From the Speed Coding Bar, create nodes or select from recently used nodes or do In-Vivo coding by selecting text and coding it with the selected text as the new node s title. From the Coder, create nodes, find nodes or view coding; code by dragging and dropping selected text to a node or a node to selected text.	
Exploring what's coded	Study how a document is coded in the Document Browser, using the Coder to highlight a node s coding passages, or Coding Stripes to line-mark in the margin where nodes code.	Study what a node codes in the Node Browser to read all passages coded, then recode or jump to a coded document to browse and edit it. To see how other nodes code this node s text, use the Coder and Coding Stripes as for documents.

CODING PROCESSES	Documents	Nodes
Revising and refining coding	In a Document or Node Browser, alter, delete or refine coding, creating or changing nodes as new categories emerge. View the context of coding passages. Spread coding as desired to wider contexts, and recode into subtler categories.	
Reporting coding	Make rich text reports of documents or nodes showing patterns of coding, statistics on coding of documents or coding at nodes.	

All the ways of organizing, linking and coding data are brought together in integrated search procedures.

SEARCHING PROCESSES	Documents	Nodes
Choosing the question: *What do you want to ask?*	Integrated Search: Text searches and Coding-based search processes are integrated, along with attribute-based search. Look for these text patterns, and/or this coding, and/or these attribute values in the same search. Choose an operation - what do you want to ask? - from four main groups of search types offering a logically complete range of searches; including, Boolean and relational searches.	
Text searching	String and Pattern searches, permitting approximation and sounds-like similarities, can be made as searches in their own right or as arguments in a relational search e.g. find "this phrase", where it occurs in "these nodes", in text coded from "documents" with these "attribute values" i.e. Scope.	
Choosing where you search: *Where do you want to ask it?*	Specify a scope of documents, and/or coding passages (nodes), and/or passages (documents and nodes) with specific attribute values. Save the Scope as a node to code that material. Or search just that material. Rerun a related search on the same material, or run the same search on a changed scope.	
Asking: *What's there?*	Ask Which questions to assay the contents of any node, set, scope, or search result. (Which age groups are represented here? Which case nodes code the data retrieved? Which documents have finds?) View Assay results in tables before searching.	
Choosing a results format: *What do you want to do with the answer?*	Specify processes and how you want results. Save results of searches as nodes, so you can ask further questions of your finds. You can assess results one by one as they are found to see if they should be kept. (You can lump all finds into one node, or keep the finds from each scope item in separate nodes, or simply record [as sets] which scope items have finds.)	

SEARCHING PROCESSES	Documents	Nodes
Qualitative matrices	Create and view a Matrix showing patterns of coding or attributes in tabular format. View on screen to see many statistical patterns in the table. Cells are "live": click to see the text coded in that cell.	
Building on search results	Use the search system again to further explore the finds from a search, building on answers to previous questions. (System closure - results are further data and available for analysis and critiquing.) Code the finds with further, perhaps more analytical, categories, to build up a theoretical analysis. Put the results into a Model to develop a visual representation of what they say.	

Items from each of the three systems of a project: documents, nodes and attributes, can be represented, linked and commented on in qualitative models that are multidimensional and layered as your theory develops.

MODELING PROCESSES	**Documents**	**Nodes**
Drawing live models	Build up a visual display in the Modeler of items you specify; documents, nodes, attributes and their relations and groupings.	
Linking models to live data	Documents, nodes and attributes are live in the model - click on their icons to inspect their data or properties. Use to explore theory, check project progress etc. Make free use of labeled links, notes, comments; layering, position and style controls to set up diagrams to your taste and purposes.	
Changing and managing models and their contents	Models and their contents are displayed in Model Explorer. Move model items around, change layout to express views of data or theory. Add or remove items, drag-and-drop into the model and out.	
Layering, styling and grouping items and links in models	Create and define styles of model links or items. Use these to distinguish different theories, actors, processes etc. Show or hide specified styles as you explore the data. Create and label layers of a model, exploring and changing them with drag-and-drop in the Model Explorer. Select, combine and show or hide layers to explore data. Group items and show or hide those groups.	

What you do with the tool-kit described above will depend on your goals.

Any NVivo project will probably involve organizing, linking, categorizing, questioning, shaping and synthesizing. These are not separate tasks, and are usually in no predetermined sequence. From the start of a project, the researcher is involved in all six. Different projects will have different emphases and use the tools differently. NVivo is designed to support integration from the commencement of the project, linking documents and nodes, combining them in questioning and supporting collation of dynamic document reports at every stage of the project. It is also designed to avoid sequencing these actions; for example, you don't have to create a finished document before coding it.

Doing it: Creating a Project

To do research with NVivo, you create a Project to hold data, observations, ideas and links between them. Any number of projects can be created, and any number of people can participate in a Project.

The New Project Wizard offers options for a "typical" project with just one user, or a custom setup.

Choosing a Typical or Custom Project

A Typical project pathway is provided for projects with only a single user, and no need for special location or different access rights. This makes it quick and simple to set up.

If this suits you, you can set up a project in seconds. The New Project Wizard takes you, by default, through that path. You name the project, optionally add a description, and the Project is created in the default Projects folder.

Each of the above properties of your project can be changed later if you wish. Other team members can also be added now or later.

Choose a Custom project if you require the Wizard to take you through extra steps to locate the project in a folder you create or choose, or to specify login access for yourself or other team members. Remember you can change these aspects of the project later.

The Wizard asks for location of the new project and then your name and password. The person creating the project is termed the Administrator.

The Administrator's role is one of housekeeping. If you are a researcher in the team, you may wish to create a team member identity for yourself to make it easier to differentiate between your role as administrator and your role as project participant.

Project Properties

A project's Properties are its name, description and the names and access rights of team members. Each of these properties can be changed later if you wish. From the properties box you can get a statistical overview of the state of the project.

Project Name

This can be up to 16 characters. It must be different from the name of any of your other projects (NVivo will check for you). The default is My Project, not usually a good name!

At any stage you can change the name of a project (for example if you whizzed through the Wizard's Typical setup too swiftly and created one called My Project!)

Password

NVivo does not require that projects be password protected, but you can use a password if you wish. This is a good idea if the data you are handling is confidential; your personal computer is unlikely to be completely private.

WARNING: The password must not be forgotten or mislaid. It cannot be recovered from the project by anyone else, even QSR! So if the password is not known, the project cannot be opened. If you set up a project with a password, keep a record of it in a secure place.

Importing a NUD*IST Project

Importing a NUD*IST4 Project into an NVivo Project is straightforward, and the areas of the NUD*IST project will appear in familiar ways in NVivo. But, note two things have happened:

1. NVivo gives memos full document status. Your memos on documents or nodes in NUD*IST4 will appear as full documents in the Document Explorer, and are given the DocLinks to make them Memos in NVivo (with the title determined accordingly e.g. "Memo for – DAVID"). The Explorer tells you whether each document or node has a memo.

2. NVivo will create a Tree node called Working Nodes as a root for nodes that are not needed in the new software. (It does not need a node for Annotations, though of course you can have one if you prefer. It is more flexible than N4 in placing the working nodes from search operations.)

NVivo will not block you importing a project twice, or importing a second project into the same NVivo project, since many researchers may want to do this. Documents and nodes with the same name are not merged; NVivo adds a numeral to one name so they can be distinguished.

How to get going in a project

Qualitative projects often start from little structure, the launching place being curiosity or hunches, awareness of a problem or a puzzle, rather than a formal hypothesis. This can be a serious problem when researchers are unable to get started, because the project seems to have no beginning.

NVivo is designed to assist researchers working from such situations, as well as those with structured project plans. There is no need to wait until the project seems orderly (it may never do so!).

You need not have any data before you create a project, and creating a project requires no previous decisions about the nature of the data. Documents can be imported or added to the project at any stage, and in many different forms. Documents can be developed inside the project.

A project can be created at any stage, but the software will assist from the earliest genesis of the project. Here are several ways of getting going; choose one, or blend them as you please, NVivo doesn't mind!

Starting with documents

Chapter 3 explains the flexibility of documents. Exploiting this flexibility will get you going quickly and maximize your gathering and use of early material. You can organize documents to suit your data and project. All documents are rich text files, but the source of the document can be text imported or created in a project. The document can also be a proxy representing files on your computer that you do not wish to import, or that are inaccessible.

- Early in a project, you can import documents as their relevance occurs, without committing to the time-consuming processes of editing. Don't worry if they're not right - NVivo's rich text editor supports any amendment later;

- If you are uncertain about the relevance of material, represent it by a Proxy Document in which you can write summaries, without the expense of scanning or transcription. You can even paste bits of the original into the Proxy as you need them;

- You may also use Proxies to represent, summarize, and annotate material you can't easily include as an on-line computer file;

- Use a Proxy document as a "vehicle" (like dough in a raisin bun) to hold DataBite links to segments (or all) of multimedia documents – or just about any computer file you can "run": pictures, spreadsheets, audio or video files, website pages – the list goes on. If you have the appropriate application programs to open these files, you can arrange for just small excerpts to appear sprinkled throughout your NVivo document. NVivo's compound documents can be built up from many different sorts of monomedia data in a flexible and economical way.

> *From the start, it is helpful to see documents as live, not dead records of "original" data. They can be changed as your understanding grows. Think of documents not as separate data containers, but as patches of data that link to each other and other things, across the project in many ways – as hyper-documents. It is a single living growing tapestry with n dimensions, not a row of inscribed gravestones.*
>
> *The live document in NVivo can be used as a changing overview of your project. A useful way to start a project is by creating a Project Document. Import or write your project plan as an NVivo document; code it at nodes for the initial, central categories this project is about. Link it to other documents that summarize discussions with your team or literature you have read, giving you immediate access to methods issues. Relate later "project-level" design and methodology documents to it with DocLinks.*

Starting with nodes

Chapter 4 explains the flexibility of nodes. As with documents, the nodes where you store ideas and categories and represent people and things in your project, can be created and changed at any time, so there is no need to delay storing of early ideas. Start with nodes for the people you will interview, for the parts of the systems you will study and for the places and institutions you will deal with. Describe them by giving them attribute values. You don't need to have any coding in them (yet … maybe ever!).

The Node Explorer allows you to reorganize, merge or delete nodes at any time, so it is not necessary to manage them logically early in a project. As ideas occur at the early stage, you can organize them as suits you. Later on, as you get data into the project, you can code it at the nodes you have already created.

- Use Free Nodes for ideas not yet belonging anywhere;

- Use the node Trees to "catalogue" categories and subcategories for easy access, like a library catalogue;

- Use Case Nodes for access to all material about each case, and case type nodes to group cases e.g. all the doctors, all the hospitals, all the suburbs. Store information on their attributes;

Starting with Sets

Sets of documents or nodes are simple to use, and a very direct way of starting to see patterns. It takes only moments to make a set. Drag the icons for the document or nodes you want into the Sets you want them to belong to. Think of Sets as friendly housekeepers. Often one of the problems early in a project is that the first data is overwhelming in its many meanings, and alarming in its tentative status. Make Sets for everything you want to think about.

Any document or node can be placed in as many sets as it belongs to (in each you place an alias, or shortcut, to the item – not the item itself). That first precious pilot interview may belong with "Experimental interviews", "Early impressions documents" and "Not yet coded".

Starting with attributes

Chapter 5 explains the uses of attributes and the ways you specify and change them and their values.

At the start of the project, you may know some things you will want to store information about: e.g. the demographic details of interviewees (age, religion, etc.), the type of interview, the size of hospital or the locations and structure of sites. Setting up these attributes early on is very simple, and may help you collect that information in an orderly fashion as documents build up. You don't even need to have any existing documents or nodes – just think of the main features you are going to want your people, interviews, historical documents and trial judgments to be categorized under, and set them up as attributes.

Don't feel committed to your first ideas. You can change your attributes as information changes.

Starting with models

Chapter 9 explains how to make and change graphical models. They can be created, altered, and deleted at any stage.

- Use the Modeler to draw your project design, as a flow chart, with nested diagrams, draft plans, detail first impressions or linking the things to do;

- Sketch early hunches, alternative theories and hypotheses; store these as layers or new models and return to compare them and change aspects in them using the Model Explorer;

- Use the Modeler to plan team roles and review team processes.

Read on...

Researchers running NVivo are invited to see it as a comprehensive and dynamic management and research package. It supports not only project data but also project specifications, project management and monitoring, data analysis and the results thereof and project reporting facilities. All these aspects can be integrated via the above-mentioned database handling, analysis and reporting facilities.

Researchers are encouraged to apply NVivo early to a project, before finalized data documents are prepared. Several non-exclusive ways of beginning and growing are described. Their overall message is that NVivo is an environment for *doing* a project – including management – not just a tool for carrying out stylized operations (such as code-and-retrieve) on the field data components of a project that exists independently of NVivo.

The following chapters explain the functions of documents, nodes, attributes, and the processes by which they are linked. Full instructions are in the *Reference Manual* (note: chapters on a topic in this book and the *Reference Manual* have the same numbers). As this chapter has shown, divisions between these topics are artificial, because in NVivo they are integrated from the start of a project. You will find there is virtually no process in NVivo which involves only one of the data types described and that the processes interlock and lead to other processes. That's what qualitative research is like! NVivo supports such integration of analysis stages and linking of processes, but it also offers powerful tools to manage the data and monitor the processes.

If you are familiar with manual or computer methods that require a document to be created in plain text, or to stay unchanged, discard those assumptions! NVivo is designed to preserve and enhance richness of records and permit any amount of change and enhancement. Using this software, you can create and handle qualitative research documents that are both rich and dynamic and connect them in many ways.

Overview:

* Documents in NVivo are in rich text and dynamic and therefore can be added to, altered and expanded as your understanding grows;

* NVivo supports compound documents, containing DataLinks to other sorts of data files (e.g. audio, video or picture) or to other documents or nodes;

* Documents can be imported or created and at any stage edited in rich text;

* Data need not be contained "in" the database, but can be represented by rich text Proxy Documents which can be edited, changed, contain textual descriptions or excerpts of the original material, contain DataLinks to any file and be coded like any other document;

* Neither the ways the document represents data (imported or a Proxy) nor the researcher's initial purpose for the document (as "original data" or as a Memo) affect the ways in which a document can be developed and used in analysis;

* Documents can be viewed, managed, and accessed by outline in the Document Explorer;

* **Document Properties** (title, description and owner) can be changed at any time;

* Any document can be edited in the Document Browser and rich text editing can be used for visual coding of documents, instead of, or complementary to, coding at nodes. Text copied from another project document will retain its rich text formatting and coding;

* Any part of a document can be coded at any number of nodes. Documents have no fixed text units, and any characters can be edited without affecting coding;

- ✦ Documents can be managed in any number of sets for access or for scoping and conducting searches;

- ✦ Any document can be made a Memo, and this property can be changed at any time. Memos are full-status documents, identified by their icons. Memos can be (but need not be) linked to other documents or particular places in documents, or to nodes. Memos (or any other group of documents) can be identified for retrieval, searching or data management;

- ✦ Documents can be given values of any number of attributes.

Go to the *Reference Manual*, Chapter 3, for instructions on how to make and manage documents in NVivo and how to edit and report on documents.

Qualitative documents: rich, dynamic, compound

Rich documents

Qualitative data is normally "rich" data, and rich data is complex, multifaceted and vivid. Qualitative data also grows as research events create records and the researcher's understanding of them changes. Such data is rarely restricted to text.

By contrast, qualitative analysis software has in the past required that documents be in plain text and relatively static.

NVivo changes this. It supports rich text and access to data of any type. You can use NVivo's rich text editor to edit any document at any stage of the project. You can use rich text for visual coding of documents, instead of, or complementary to, coding at nodes. Documents need no longer be uniform "monomedia", but can be compound.

Compound documents: qualitative linking

The software supports a variety of methods of linking documents and ideas. DataLinks are hyperlinks to other sorts of data and can be placed anywhere in a document. DataBites are links which take you to annotations or other files in any media. DocLinks take you to other documents in the project and NodeLinks to nodes where coding categories and the pointers to the coded data are stored. *(Linking is discussed in Chapter 6.)*

Memos: full status documents

Qualitative research usually requires that the data and the growing understanding be interwoven. Keeping memos is central to some methods, particularly grounded theory. This is done by linking records of research events (field notes, transcripts of interviews, etc.) with each other and with records of subsequent interpretation and discovery (memos, diaries, research notes, etc.)

In the past software has imposed a distinction between "original" data and "memos". Memos were treated as add-on documents, with limited editing and not available for coding and searching. NVivo radically removes the distinction between data and ideas: Memos are full status documents.

Coding combined with editing

Qualitative research usually involves coding and searching of coding. There are many methods of coding, but the one hitherto supported by computers has been to place references to text at categories for thinking about and gathering data. Coding has been the most obvious success of qualitative computing, but software has usually offered coding as an alternative to rich text and editing. *(See Chapter 11 or the methodological issues.)*

NVivo combines coding, editing and linking of documents with no order imposed or different modes required. Documents can be coded in many ways, and coding is not affected by editing.

Coding can be done visually in the Document Browser (see below), or can be done by placing references to text at nodes. Given the ability to import and edit rich text and to link text and other data sources, project documents or nodes, researchers are no longer restricted to coding as the only way of connecting data. The present chapter discusses editing and visual coding. *(Node coding is discussed in Chapter 7.)*

Types of documents

Documents in NVivo are classless in the sense that all sorts of documents may be handled using the same methods of adaptation and analysis.

The process of starting and changing documents can be approached in different ways, to support different methods. (It's useful to think of starting a document, rather than "creating" it, as the latter term implies a more finished product!) But neither the ways the document represents data (whether rich text is imported or a Proxy made for other data), nor the researcher's purposes ("original data" or memo), determines the ways in which a document can develop and be used in analysis.

The New Document Wizard offers three ways of starting a document. Each results in a rich text file:

♦ The full document is imported, i.e. copied, from a rich or plain text readable file into NVivo's database: You can then edit, code and search it in NVivo;

♦ The full document is represented by a Proxy Document. Specify whether it represents data on the computer or nonfile data, and how you want this document formatted. You edit, code and search it in NVivo;

♦ You create a document and edit, code and search it in NVivo.

Thus *any NVivo document, no matter how it was created*, can be enriched, explored, annotated, linked, coded, managed, searched and retrieved. A Proxy Document is not a different *sort of* data item from the document whose rich text you imported from your word processor, or the document you created in NVivo's editor. The chapters in this book each concern all sorts of documents.

If you see documents in NVivo as classless, you will find more inventive ways to represent your data.

Summary of document sources, processes and uses

	INTERNAL DOCUMENT	**PROXY DOCUMENT**
What's the document in the Project?	Copy of the data record. Rich text, directly imported or created in the NVivo editor.	Proxy Document for a file either elsewhere on your computer or not accessible. It optionally records the units of the source document.
How was it created and added to the project?	Importing a file created in a word processor as rich text or plain text; imported via the New Document Wizard or created using NVivo's editor.	Proxy created via the New Document Wizard; user specifies where or what the source document is and optionally defines numbered paragraphs representing the contents of that source document.
What can you do with the document?	The document is editable and can be browsed; any characters can be coded visually and at nodes. Its text can be printed out with or without coding displayed. Any document can be given the values of Attributes and can be placed in Sets. Paragraph units can be pre-formatted for coding in a Proxy document to represent units of the data item (parts of video, pages of book etc.).	
What can you link with it?	Any document can become a Compound document by inserting DataBites linking to annotations, or other files, (e.g. illustrate with sound or graphic segments) or hyperlinks to other documents (DocLinks) or nodes (NodeLinks).	
Why would you use this option?	Maximizes richness and fluidity of dynamic documents and detail of retrieval. Preferred option if document is text and accessible.	Allows rich and detailed interpretative version to grow even when full document is not imported. Preferred option when source is unwieldy, not text or inaccessible.
EXAMPLE:	Imported document is field notes or tape transcript. Study, edit and code on screen. Document grows with inserts to represent full account of the event.	Proxy for tape of focus group: transcribe moderator's notes, insert interpretation, links and illustrations. Proxy may become the live report for presentation.

Choosing the type of document

You choose whether to import or create the document or make a proxy, according to the sorts of data being handled and your goals for analysis.

Reasons for importing the text

- Importing a readable file is the preferred option for text documents that are accessible on the computer, since the fullest possible detail is available to inform character-based on screen coding and linking.

- Importing is very quick. The rich text format (.rtf) or text (.txt) file can be imported directly. NVivo takes the title of the document, its header and subheaders as instructed from the text.

Reasons for using a Proxy

- The research timetable is very short, and analysis goals do not require full transcription of data, making this an efficient way of maximizing interpretation and minimizing clerical work;

- The data is easily represented in units for coding and annotating. A compound document will represent many aspects of the original data better than a monomedia document. It may incorporate partial transcript, interpretive comments, and DataBites linking to the nontext data files of audio, picture or video records. For example, a focus group document might start as the moderator's memory-based summary, with DataBites leading to sound clips of significant discussion stages. As the tape is reviewed, the summary can be developed and enhanced with other images or sound clips, fuller transcription and DataBite annotations;

- The full document is very large or not accessible, (e.g. a major report): the proxy can contain a summary or notes with numbered paragraphs for pages or chapters, and notes edited into the appropriate places and coded. This is particularly appropriate to historical research;

- Proxy Documents provide a medium for new ways of storing data. For example, you might have a proxy for an informant, who provides material during field research; use that document as a vehicle for links to all their notes, films of their observations etc.

Any of the above data types may be represented in a compound document for reporting. A researcher whose use of the focus group is for an oral presentation to a team or a client, rather than detailed transcript-based analysis, might present exactly this rich and dynamic document as the conclusion of that project sector. The Proxy is a vehicle for illustrations and links to other data and models.

External Documents in N4 represent external data, and can be coded and have memos, but have no textual representation in the database. If you have used external documents it is worth rethinking the ways you could use a file that now is linked to the external data.

Reasons for making the document in NVivo's editor

Why not?! NVivo has its own rich text editor. Any document you are creating and changing during a project can start this way.

Documents are dynamic in NVivo, not frozen as in other manual or some computer methods. Data you previously kept in notebooks or jottings can grow and be managed in the database. Type research diaries, field notes, project rethinks and audit reports into the NVivo editor, just as you would in a word processor. Edit and add to it as the ideas grow, or as you decide to embellish an early brief account. If you are typing it directly into NVivo, you can annotate and add DataLinks as they occur to you. You can code as you go, creating categories and doing coding as the document grows.

Designing the Document System

There are very few rules governing the setting up of a document system. If you have worked with qualitative software, you will benefit from challenging the assumptions previously required.

Designing for editable documents

In designing the ways you will handle data, think editing. In NVivo, editing and coding are not two distinct processes. If you are used to coding with previous qualitative software, you will not have exploited the ability to edit, since the two were incompatible.

Qualitative researchers require the ability to change rich data as ideas emerge and understanding grows. NVivo's support for editing and coding means that you can revise, expand and comment upon documents. This allows you to visually code during, or as an alternative to, coding at nodes.

If you are upgrading from NUD*IST4 you are familiar with its ability to support coding of *changing* documents by editing, deleting, inserting and annotating of text whilst *maintaining the accuracy of coding*. But the fixed text units of N4 meant that changes were restricted to adding, altering or deleting particular text units. This is not the case in NVivo, where any number of characters may be selected, deleted, altered or inserted at any place in the text.

No need for sameness

Documents do not need to be homogeneous in NVivo, and heterogeneous documents do not mean the project will fall apart. Most qualitative projects require and build up a heterogeneous body of data, often with variety not anticipated at the start of the project.

Sets and attributes, as well as coding, allow you to make sense of variety. For example:

◆ If early data records transcribe easily in rich text, but later ones are more unwieldy or the budget more challenging, you can use proxy documents as their containers. Make a set of all Proxy Documents so you can filter them out of searches where you want full transcripts.

◆ If the pilot interviews are transcribed in full to establish the range of issues to be considered, but later material is recorded in note form, create a document attribute "record detail" with values for different levels of detail. You can then assess analysis stages in terms of the detail of data supporting them.

Compound documents for new purposes

Starting a project does not require starting many documents. Once you discover the potential of documents that are "live", editable and linkable, you might start a project quite differently. This will affect the sequences and timing of the project, as well as the richness of analysis. New sorts of documents are supported by the functions outlined above. In particular, many projects may be helped by starting with an Audit Document or a Project Document. *(See Chapter 11, Getting it Together)*

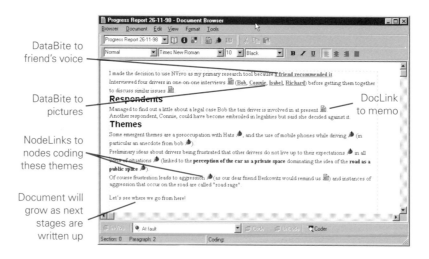

DataBite to friend's voice

DataBite to pictures

NodeLinks to nodes coding these themes

Document will grow as next stages are written up

DocLink to memo

Starting Documents

Starting a document is simple. The New Document Wizard offers three ways
– locate and import a readable file, make a Proxy or make a new document in
NVivo's Editor. The Wizard steps you through the fastest route possible to
determine source, name, description and location. Note: it is not necessary to
import documents one at a time. Full instructions are in the *Reference Manual*.

Importing a rich text file

NVivo will import a rich text (.rtf) file from MS Word or from Wordpad,
which comes in the Accessories folder of Microsoft Windows. It will also
import a plain text (.txt) file from any word processor. The rich text file will
retain color, font, emphasis and levels of headings. NVivo provides a rich
text editor with which you can alter or add all these rich text features to
existing files, or write new files using them. (See *Reference Manual, Appendix
A: Document Preparation.*)

NVivo takes the title of the document, its description and subheaders as
instructed from the text. You can have the document's name and description
allocated automatically in any of three ways – or you can just type them in. If
you selected either of the options where no file is readable (a Proxy for
nonfile data or a new document) NVivo will ask for the name and
description. For the Proxy it will also ask for type and location of the source
being represented (you can select from a drop-down list of possible sources
of data or type in another, which will be added to the list).

> *To minimize the clerical work of importing, set and stick to a routine,
> whereby, for example, the source file name becomes the document name
> and the first paragraph becomes the description (the first option) or the first
> paragraph the name and the second the description. Names and descriptions
> can be altered after the document is imported – as can any other part of the
> document.*

Using rich text for impact

It may be hard to (re)learn to exploit rich text if you are experienced with a
qualitative computing package. Researchers used to writing in rich text in
word processors were previously forced to accept plain text for code based
retrieval in qualitative computing. In NVivo, the rich text capacity can be
used exactly as it is in word processors, to give emphasis, indicate ownership
of different sections, differentiate comment from observation, convey
different levels of importance. But it can also be used for specific purposes
in NVivo:

If you have previously used plain text, it is worth reviewing the purposes to
which you could utilize a variety of fonts, colors etc. In a transcript of a
focus group, color might visually identify different themes, a different font

the comments of the moderator: underlining and bold could be used to indicate <u>emphasis</u> or **importance**. Imported into NVivo, the transcript can be viewed exactly in this form, and aspects of the rich text changed on screen. The Explorer shows heading levels in an outline display which allows you to mark questions and speaker identifiers as headings then click on one to go there directly.

If rich text is unfamiliar, ask how it might be used to do tasks hitherto accomplished by coding (see "Visual Coding", below). In NVivo, coding, editing and linking will usually be combined; these are no longer separate processes!

Using headings and subheadings

Up to nine levels of subheadings in the rich text file are recognized by NVivo. They may be added or edited after import of a document. But the time of creation or transcription of a document is often the most useful time for inserting subheadings, whilst the tone of voice, the background happenings, or the immediacy of the event are clear to the researcher. If you insert them then you can auto-code with them (see below).

In NVivo you can use subheadings for any of the reasons you use them in a word processor:

 ♦ They delineate subsections - themes, stages in an argument, developments in a process;

 ♦ They shape your document and make it more easily viewed. Records of participant observation, for example, are clearer if sequences of events are set out with subheadings;

 ♦ Multilayered documents benefit from using *many levels* of subheadings. For example, in a group discussion the questions by the moderator might be level 2 headings, the speaker identifiers heading level 3, and particular topics identified by that speaker heading level 4.

There are also reasons for using subheadings that are particular to NVivo and its ways of handling access to text, coding and retrieval:

 ♦ Subheadings define different levels of Sections in the document. You can spread to sections the context of coding in the Node Browser, or results from searches. Thus in the group discussion document described above, you could search for every occurrence of a phrase, then ask to retrieve the whole of each *speech* in which it occurred (level 3), or the whole of the *discussion of a question* by several speakers (level 2);

 ♦ Spreading to sections allows you to use the search procedures to "auto-code" – sending NVivo to find a phrase or pattern of coding and then return the whole section it occurs in;

- NVivo's Section Coder will auto-code the specified sections in a document. This is a considerable time-saver for handling data that can be structured in sections. If you wish to use subheadings for auto-coding, please go to instructions for formatting documents and use of the Section Coder in the *Reference Manual*.

- An outline of headings is shown in the Document Explorer, (right hand side when the document is selected) and provides an important new means of reviewing and accessing documents in NVivo. Select any subheading and click Browse to jump directly to that subheading in the document.

Making a Proxy Document:

If you elected to create a Proxy, you will be asked to specify whether this is file or non-file data, (if it's on file, you are asked to locate it). NVivo will create a rich text file for this document. The options that follow will be concerned with making a format for the data to assist the researcher with coding and locating commentary or DataLinks. If you don't want to bother with a format, make a blank rich text file.

Why format?

Formatting of proxy documents is designed to assist the swift handling of certain types of data. Proxy documents can contain as many numbered paragraphs as required to represent any data, for example, page numbers, tape counts, the rooms of a building or years in a journal. You can fill out this skeleton as you wish, with summaries, comments, or excerpts of the data they represent. This can be done either as text or as DataBite links to other files, including audio visual. You can then transcribe as little or as much as you want of, for example, focus group data, whilst tracking where themes occurred. You can delete numbered paragraphs, of course, if you decide these parts of the document are not relevant.

Having the units of data pre-specified will assist if you are handling data by proxy that will require detailed annotation, summary, coding or linking. For example:

- Preformat proxies to represent large documents where a précis of each unit (e.g. chapter of a report) must be typed in. Make the units in the Proxy chapters, and when reviewing the Proxy you will be reminded which ones have as yet no précis;

- Formatting helps keep track of coding in documents that will be coded in fine detail of units (e.g. a videotape) with DataLinks frequently inserted (e.g. to sound bites or images from the tape). Make the units the tape count numbers, type your summaries in the relevant places, locating

DataBites to the tape in the summary. Formatting means that even though the whole document may not be on the screen, you can still see the patterns of your coding of particular units displayed in the margin coding stripes.

If you decide to use formatting, reflect on the layout of your Proxy Document and the way it would best represent its source. For example, to have units as page numbers for that large report is probably quite unnecessary (you can insert exact references in the summary) whilst pages would be most useful for a proxy representing a salient journal article.

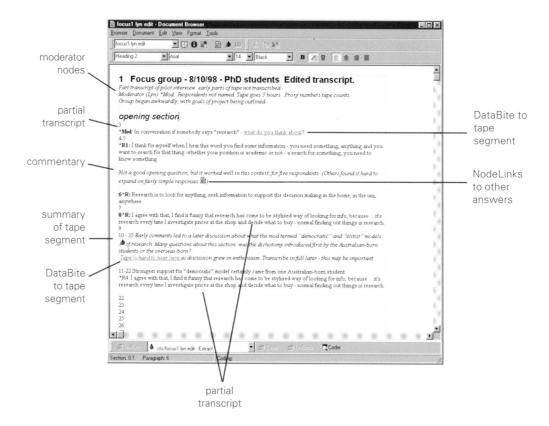

moderator nodes

partial transcript

commentary

summary of tape segment

DataBite to tape segment

DataBite to tape segment

NodeLinks to other answers

partial transcript

Starting (and continuing) by editing documents

The final Wizard option for starting a document is to create a new document. If you select this option, a Document Browser opens on the new document. (Similarly, you create a new document if you place a DocLink and ask to create a new document to link to.) Any document, no matter how it is started in your project, can be continued in this way.

The ability to create and edit documents supports new research techniques. Perhaps a key informant has acquired significance: start a document noting this relationship and add to it as the project progresses, linking it to all the data about this person and deriving from them. Perhaps a paper or report is to be prepared – start it as an NVivo document, with links to the data to be described. Dynamic documents have many such roles to play.

> *If you are starting or growing a document in the Browser, experiment with coding as you go. Get in the habit of using rich text editing for visual coding (see below). Explore how the In-Vivo code button makes a node titled with the text you highlight. For example, if you are creating a new document by writing up field notes, as you write, highlight the words for major issues raised and create free nodes for them, coding the relevant context. Check out the Explorer functions of the Coder: you could make Case Nodes for all the people attending that event, and code what you write about them, as you write it up.*

Starting by importing a NUD*IST4 project

Documents can be directly imported from a NUD*IST4 project, with all coding and properties they had in that project.

If you import an N4 project, all documents will appear in the NVivo project. Your imported plain text documents in N4 can contain subheadings. These will be given level one heading status on import to NVivo, so you can immediately view their outline in the Document Explorer and select the relevant sections to Browse. The document is of course now editable in rich text, including selecting and setting other headings to define subsections. You may wish to insert DataBites immediately to link with other files that were not in the N4 project.

All memos will be full documents – now you are confronted with their presence, you may wish to delete some of them, or copy them into annotations as DataBites *(see Chapter 7)*.

If you have worked previously in NUD*IST4, you will be familiar with the distinction between imported and external files. NVivo develops this feature by providing the Proxy document, pre-formatted, for external files. Upon import, your external files in N4 will become Proxy Documents in NVivo, with paragraphs numbered, so coding will be correct.

Editing Documents

Using the Rich Text Editor

NVivo's editor is available for editing any readable text file, whether or not it is in a Project document, and whether or not you are in a project.

Call the NVivo editor to open any rich text or plain text file in an edit window. It will open any readable file, that is a Microsoft Word or WordPad .rtf file, or a .txt file from any word processor.

Editing in the Document Browser

Text editing functions are found, as is usual in word processors, on the top bar of the window and in its Tools and Format menu. Some are duplicated on the context (right mouse button) menu for swift access whilst you are typing. You can use these to set and change the style, font, size and color of selected text. Nine heading levels are available, along with Description and Title styles. The Browser, however, is not merely a rich text editor. It has the following features designed for qualitative data handling:

- You can select another document in the slot on the top bar, and the Browser will switch to that document – a useful way to move between documents while reviewing them;

- Like the Explorers, both the Document Browser and the Node Browser carry icons on their toolbars giving access to Browse (to open other documents as well), Properties, Report, Attributes, DocLinks and NodeLinks;

- The Document Browser is also a window for coding! As you write a document, or edit one, you can also code, either by editing in Visual Coding (see below) or by coding at nodes, using either the Speed Coding Bar at the bottom, or the Coder. *(See Chapter 7)*

> *Note that NVivo's Document Browser combines editing and coding by restricting the ability to overwrite highlighted text. This prevents accidental deletion of, or replacement of, text you intend to code! When text is highlighted use the delete button if you really mean to delete it.*

If you are not used to editing qualitative data, play with its potential for aesthetic effect, as well as for more formal methodological purposes. Qualitative research requires ability to focus on text, see patterns, hold onto hunches, locate things half heard, and avoid boredom even when the data at face value is boring. Rich text is a great advantage for these purposes. But most significantly, in supporting rich text, NVivo supports a form of coding long unavailable to qualitative research.

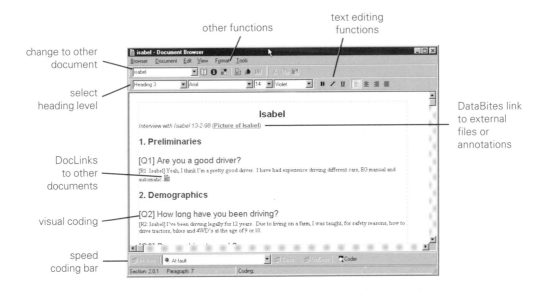

Visual coding

Rich text in NVivo provides for visual ways of identifying data passages, by color, highlighting or different text style and by annotation.

These are hardly radical methods: they were the prime means of *marking up* data handled without computers. They never had a label – they were just what researchers did to text. Here they are termed visual coding, to distinguish them from the now usual coding that is done on computer by storing references, or pointers, to (usually plain) text at nodes. "Coding", when unqualified, will refer to node coding.

The advantages and disadvantages of the two ways NVivo supports coding, visual and node, are discussed in Chapter 7.

Using font, color and style for visual coding

As a document is created in the word processor or in NVivo, use color, font, bold and italic for whatever purpose you wish. Or as you read text, change it in the Document Browser by selecting text and altering color, font etc.

You may wish to keep a key of the text characteristics you are using for different purposes. In a simple project, just keep a document called Visual Coding, and record there, for example, that purple means problems. If your visual coding becomes more complex (as it may, for example, in fine analysis of discourse) you might keep several documents on this method, and have them in a Set called "Visual Coding" for easy access.

When to use visual coding:

If you are unsure about using visual coding, consider how you might use color or font:

- Early in a project, for identifying text that raises tentative ideas, or for all those passages you don't know how to code but are sure are important;

- In a project researching the fine nuances of discourse, use color and font to indicate hesitations, moods, double meanings etc.;

- As a first stage whilst getting ideas together, to avoid creating nodes unnecessarily – return and node code the colored text once the categories firm;

- In a very small or brief project about a limited number of issues, simply color or change the font of the text to show their occurrence. For example, a focus group setting agendas for a policy change, might be colored to show the issues raised and the text italicized where there were disagreements. This rich document forms the basis for feedback and discussion;

- For categories that don't seem "nodeworthy", just things that are interesting or possibly significant;

- For the finer distinctions you might make within a category – use node coding for the main categories of the project and see the differences in the Node Browser;

- For showing behaviors and attitudes of respondents during their interviews;

- For identifying your own inserted commentary so it stands out from the other text. (Use different colors for comments of different team members).

DataBites can be used for visually coding anything you want to comment on or to link with any other file. Consider how you might use DataBites for the between-the-lines commentary in your project:

- For detailed annotation of text, if you do not want your annotations to intrude in the text as it appears on screen or in reports. Commenting on field notes or discourse commonly needs such annotation;

- For reflections on the content of the text by researchers; you might want to alter these as the data builds up or store reflections by several team members, but not have them show when the text is viewed;

- For linking the document to other files of commentary, for example an audio file of discussion of this issue or a picture of a model from NVivo.

Managing documents

NVivo is designed to allow as much or as little management of data as you wish. You can view and review all your documents in the Document Explorer. You can group them for easy monitoring or for subtle analysis by making Sets of documents. You can get access to just those documents if you wish using Sets, Attributes or Coding.

Using the Document Explorer

The Document Explorer provides direct ways of seeing, exploring and managing documents. It is the control-tower managing your flights with documents. It shows all your documents in a form similar to that of the Windows Explorer in MS Windows 95 and similar operating systems; documents acting rather like files and document groupings acting like folders. It shows recently used documents and sets of documents, and gives immediate information about them and access to them or their particular parts, as well as control of document properties. Many of these functions are new and offer significant data management facilities.

The Document Explorer, and symmetrically, the Node Explorer, also have icons on the toolbar that take you to Browse, Properties, Report, Attributes, DocLinks and NodeLinks. Full instructions are in the *Reference Manual*.

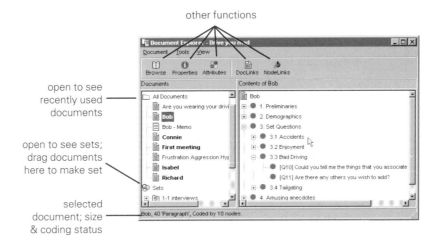

Using the Document outline

You can view the outline of a document's Sections, defined by heading levels, in the right pane. Subheadings open if you click on a heading.

Select any level of heading and click Browse to jump to the document, with the Browser open at that heading. Use this to view documents in summary, and to go directly to the section of interest.

> *Remember these are editable documents – and exploit this facility! Thus when hunger drives you to interrupt a coding session before reaching the end of a document, you might insert a level one heading "CODED TO HERE". On your return, simply open the outline in the Document Explorer, and select that heading, click Browse and you are back at the right place to renew coding.*

Making Document Sets

Integrated throughout the analysis processes of NVivo are the ways of using sets of documents and nodes. When you make a set you place at it aliases (or shortcuts) to the documents you want to group together. Think sets whenever you want to pull your documents into shape. They may be structures in the research design or entirely temporary ways of seeing the data differently.

You can make document sets immediately in the Explorer. Drag a document to the sets icon to start a new set, or drag and drop into an existing set (copy and paste works just as well). Create and build up sets of documents this way. Name them usefully, use them for temporary as well as long term tasks. Make a set of documents from each team member. Make a set to ask questions about just some documents (do any of the ones I haven't coded mention this person?). For more subtle purposes, create and change sets through the Set Editor, which allows you to select and filter exactly which documents go into a Set.

The uses of sets in managing documents and accessing them in analysis are described in *Chapter 8, Shaping Data - Sets and Trees.*

Using Document Properties

The name and description of the document can be viewed and changed at any time.

Using the name and description

When a document is imported or created it can have both a name and a description. Note the New Document Wizard offers options for automatically creating a name and description from the imported file. When you specify the name of a document its length is not restricted, but very long names will impede scanning of lists. Choice of name can usefully indicate a document's content or context.

> *NVivo lists documents in alphabetical order. Consider this in naming documents if you wish to determine their order of appearance when you select documents from lists for coding, browsing or deleting.*

Using icon color

From the Properties box you can also change the color of the document's icon. Like many functions in NVivo, this apparently cosmetic touch can be methodologically useful. The icon is displayed in the Document Explorer, Sets Editor and also in Models, thus changing icon color may help you visualize your data. Or it might simply help you enjoy the sense of control over your growing body of data and ideas, and sense that you are getting somewhere!

> *Feel free to use visual effects like icon color for functions particular to your project – or just for fun. This is how researchers worked before computers turned text gray and shapeless. Why not color red-for-danger those documents you have not yet reviewed and coded, or living-green the memos that seem to be growing into good theories, (demote them to brown when they become less convincing) or stereotypically pink and blue respectively the interviews with mothers whose babies were female and male! It's your project, these are your documents, and the software's tools are there for you to use in achieving your research goals.*

Deleting, expanding and duplicating documents

Documents need not be fixed or frozen in NVivo, indeed they are highly unlikely to be so.

Deleting a document

You can delete documents at any time. When you attempt to delete a document a warning message appears, checking that you wish to delete it, with all its properties, attributes and coding.

> *Note if you say OK, you do not delete the nodes at which it was coded, or the attributes and values that applied. Thus you might start a second project with the nodes from a first, by copying the first project, renaming the copy and deleting the documents from it. Now you have a node shell into which you can bring new documents. This might be useful for a comparative project, or to test interpretations by theoretical sampling.*

Expanding a document

The ability to edit the document (whether imported or Proxy) means that it can be expanded indefinitely. If you have been using software in which editing affects coding of subsequent text, it is important to understand that this does not occur in NVivo. Indeed if you have coding displays in place as you edit, you will see them adjust immediately.

> In order to support editing with coding, NUD*IST4 required predefined units of text. If you are used to NUD*IST4's ability to edit and add or remove whole text units after the document is in the project, you will find a new flexibility in being able to edit any characters directly. Note that whereas in N4 text has to be inserted text unit by text unit, NVivo will accept character by character text editing in any part of a document.

NVivo's editor allows you to copy text from one document to another. If the document copied is in NVivo, rich text will be copied, as will coding of nodes. Text copied from a document in another application will paste as plain text. You can of course then use NVivo's editor to add or restore rich text features (subheaders etc.) as you wish.

Text can be pasted at any place in the document. One common need in qualitative research is to append one document to another. For example, a document in the project may record an interview which was discussed with the respondent in a subsequent conversation; your notes from that discussion should be appended, so the research event can be analyzed as one document, with common attributes etc.

> If you have used the ability to Append one document to another in N4, you will find no equivalent menu item in NVivo. There is no special procedure for appending documents, since a document can just keep growing as you type or paste more text (wherever you like).

Note that pasted text becomes part of the document, so it will inherit values of attributes assigned to the document into which it is pasted. Its coding at nodes will be copied.

Duplicating documents

Any document can be duplicated. The duplicate will be identical to the original (rich text, DataLinks, properties, coding) but of course, not in name. It will have a new name, "Copy of [original name]" and a new creation date.

There are many reasons why you may wish to duplicate a document, especially in the environment of rich text editing and with the ability to change the contents of a document. For example:

◆ Retaining an original version whilst editing, commenting upon or severely cutting the duplicate copy. The original may later be deleted, if this was a safety measure;

- Originals might be kept of all documents, to compare the intact starter text with the edited version, or for perusal by another observer for auditing purposes. Duplicate pertinent documents and archive in Sets at transition points in the project. Use the coding and attribute filters in the Sets Editor and Search Tool to explore the differences between documents at different stages;

- Consistency of coding can be checked if each member of the team codes a copy and the coding is then compared visually (using coding stripes) or in summary (using reports).

> *When handling duplicate documents, it is of course, highly important to be able to distinguish them from the originals. As in many NVivo strategy areas, the choice is to do so by sets, attributes or coding. Making a set of originals and a set of duplicate documents (or perhaps sets at different stages) may be the most visual way to distinguish them. Or code them at a node for "duplicate" or the value of an attribute "duplicate". Each of these strategies allows that in any analysis you can ask a question about the original texts and compare with what happened to the duplicate.*

Memos

In NVivo Memos are not a different type of document. As most qualitative texts recommend, memos are treated as full status data.

Qualitative researchers usually spend some time storing ideas, insights, interpretations, growing understanding or recognition of puzzles that have to be understood. How these are kept and accessed is important in research design. What to do with these records of thinking?

In many methods, notably grounded theory, phenomenology and discourse analysis, such thinking is not separate from the data. Documents grow as they are interpreted. Researchers edit text, jot ideas in margins, write discussions of research issues and note things they see on the back of transcripts. If this is the way you want to work, you can exploit the rich text capacity of NVivo to edit, color and the capacity to place DataLinks in any document to annotations and other files, and to documents and nodes *(see Chapter 6)*.

Some researchers also wish to write analytic, methodological or theoretical "memos" and keep them separate from, but linked to, the data records that come from research events such as interviews or observation. Those memos grow, are themselves data, and can often be the most important of the data documents, for example, in ethnographic studies

In all qualitative techniques, manual or computer, memos have usually been restricted as add-on items. Whether they are on yellow stickits that fall off the transcript, or files in a separate computer directory, they were treated literally as afterthoughts – thoughts that come subsequent to the data documents. Because of this they are lower status, cannot be explored, annotated, coded, searched or rethought using the techniques applied to the "real data". This distinction between data and ideas is highly problematic in some methods, and an outright nuisance in all methods.

document explorer
shows memos with
separate icons

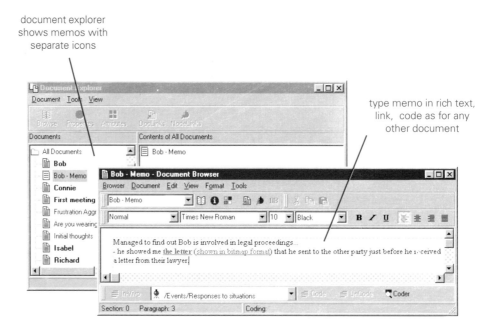

type memo in rich text,
link, code as for any
other document

Making and using memos

A Memo is a normal document. To create it use any of the usual ways of creating documents described above. Alternatively, place a DocLink (at a document, any place in its text or a node) and ask to create a new document *(See Chapter 6)*. Any number of memos may be placed at a DocLink.

Label the document a memo simply by clicking the Memo box in window when creating a document or making a DocLink. To make an existing document a memo, click Memo in the Properties window. Its icon will be changed to show that it has this status.

The memo will appear in your Document Explorer (which will show its memo status). All the facilities of the Document Explorer and Document Browser are available.

If you import a project from N4 to NVivo, all memos for documents or nodes in that project will become full documents and be given Memo status and titles which include the document or node they are attached to.

Memos and DocLinks

Memos need not be linked to any other document or node. You may want to have a memo about your changing use of qualitative methods. It could start as an unlinked document, and as you reflect on research episodes, be linked to the data records from them. If you wish to link memos to other documents, you can do so, by any of the DataLink processes discussed in Chapter 6.

Often researchers start a project with documents that are memos about their goals, or theoretical approaches. In NVivo such Memos can be stand-alone documents, clearly labeled as memos. They can be given coding or attributes to identify them and later be linked by DocLinks and NodeLinks to subsequent documents (which may themselves be memos) during the development of goals and theories.

When you create a DocLink for a document, node or text passage, the DocLinks window allows you to link that item to an existing document, or you can link the item to a new memo. If you choose to make a new memo, a Document Browser opens for you to type or copy in text. The new document is provisionally titled with the name of the document from which you are making the link, e.g. "David – Memo". (This title can of course be changed.) The new document will appear in the Document Explorer – this is indeed a way of creating a document. As for any document, you can store information about its attributes, it can be coded as richly as required and it need not be called a Memo or given that status and icon.

Remember:

♦ A Memo need not be linked to any other document or node;

♦ A DocLink can link to a document that is not a Memo (in most projects, many such links will be made). There is no need to label any, let alone all, such documents Memos.

What you can do with memos

Since a memo is a full status document, this section is rather redundant! But we are so used to treating memos as second rate documents that readers may be helped by pointers to some of the new things they can do with the records of their thinking about data.

♦ The memo can be viewed, browsed and edited in rich text, just like any other document. Memos can grow as your ideas grow;

♦ You can edit with color, font etc. to note stages in your thinking, levels of hesitation or to insert disagreements with your senior colleague;

♦ Like any other document, its icon color can be changed – use this for instant recognition of each colleague's memos, or ones that are inspiring;

- You can copy into the memo any passage you wish to discuss (from a document in your NVivo project or any other document on your computer;

- Like any other document, a memo can have memos (or other documents or nodes) linked to it at any place, with DocLinks and NodeLinks as described in Chapter 6. This means memos need no longer be dead-ends, the place your thinking stops. Depending on your methodological goals, they can become webs of thinking, linked and linking-to other material;

- A memo can of course have the values of attributes. Note that these include date/time attributes which have considerable significance for memo review and auditing of the development of theory. Give memos date values and you can later review all the memos you wrote *after* you read that mind-blowing new book, or *before* the conflict in management of the company studied became public;

- Memos can be coded, visually or at nodes, by any of the processes described in Chapter 7. Thus you can use the full range of search procedures described in Chapter 10. (Give me all the text in Memos coded at conflict in management and also at opposition to your study, if they were written before the public exposure of conflict);

- Memos can be managed in sets. There is no limit to the number of sets a document may be aliased to. The system keeps a set of all memos, but you might wish to have many other sets, for example, one for each researcher in a team. All the search and analysis processes apply to it as to any other document.

How to identify memos in analysis procedures

Given the ability to treat memos as full status data, many researchers may not wish to differentiate them in analysis. The distinction between "raw" data and ideas is in many methods an anathema. In others (for example historical research) it is central.

The system stores a set of all memos for such questions as: "Let's review all my own notes about the behavior of the male members of the group observed", or "What evidence do I have that the people interviewed saw doctors' authority as problematic – as opposed to my own commentary that they did?" In all the access and analysis procedures described in this book, the researcher can restrict a process to, or exclude from it, everything in a Set or Sets. In all the processes with sets, you can use the filter in the Sets Editor to select only the documents you want to have in a set for your current purpose. *(See Chapter 8.)*

You can click and clear the box making a document a Memo at any time; thereby changing its icon and defining it in or out of the Set.

> *If your memos are not whole documents, but brief annotations or insertions, you can identify these by coding at a node for annotations. N4 projects contained this option. Since NVivo provides the 'hidden' annotations at DataBites, an Annotation node is not provided - but you might like to create one.*

Should it be a Memo?

Memo status is not unchangeable in NVivo. DocLinks support Memos to other documents in the project at any place in a document or at a node. Thus DocLinks offer a new ability to link any document at relevant places to other data. Whether you choose to differentiate memos is up to you. Different methods carry very different attitudes to the separation of data and thinking about it: you choose according to your goals.

If you are used to writing Memos and seeing them as add-on documents with lesser status, you may wish to keep working that way, expanding your use of memos gradually as you adapt familiar techniques to take advantage of NVivo's options.

Note that you can, however, immediately broaden your methods to use DocLinks to other documents that are not memos. For example, you might link two interviews with Sam, or the interview with him and what he said in a focus group. This is unlikely to be or become a Memo by you about the event (though you might wish to edit in a note about the differences in these accounts – and perhaps code that note at your node for Memos).

Since this document (the brief interview) has no lesser status, you can edit, (in rich text) code, and link it. There is no limit to the levels of links-within-linked documents. DocLinks allow linking, for example, to a summary of a book, or to notes on a particular theory. A document might start as a reflection on the document to which it is linked and grow to reflect on many documents, or on ideas at nodes. Go to the DocLinks window and add those new links. *(See Chapter 6.)*

Profiles and Reports of Documents

Documents, and their links and coding, can be profiled on the screen and reported on out of NVivo. There is a wide range of report output options, including counts of items and coding, and displays of coding. These are fully outlined in the *Reference Manual,* Chapter 11.

You can display (and print) profiles of documents. A profile is a table of data whose content you specify. For example, you might wish all the field notes profiled by events recorded, or the values of the age attribute. Profile tables give clear, graphical representation of the breakdown of your data records on coding or attributes. Export if you wish to a graphics package or spreadsheet.

You can print from the Document Browser, or make and print all reports from NVivo. Print the Browser displays of documents with their coding stripes and numbered paragraphs and sections, and the DataBite annotations as endnotes. Create comprehensive rich-text reports to list information on all areas of your project, for editing in NVivo, saving or printing.

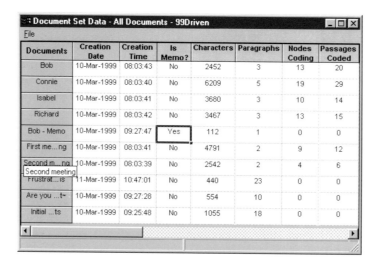

Documents	Creation Date	Creation Time	Is Memo?	Characters	Paragraphs	Nodes Coding	Passages Coded
Bob	10-Mar-1999	08:03:43	No	2452	3	13	20
Connie	10-Mar-1999	08:03:40	No	6209	5	19	29
Isabel	10-Mar-1999	08:03:41	No	3680	3	10	14
Richard	10-Mar-1999	08:03:42	No	3467	3	13	15
Bob - Memo	10-Mar-1999	09:27:47	Yes	112	1	0	0
First me...ng	10-Mar-1999	08:03:41	No	4791	2	9	12
Second m...ng	10-Mar-1999	08:03:39	No	2542	2	4	6
Frustrat...is	11-Mar-1999	10:47:01	No	440	23	0	0
Are you ...t~	10-Mar-1999	09:27:28	No	554	10	0	0
Initial ...ts	10-Mar-1999	09:25:48	No	1055	18	0	0

Document Set Data - All Documents - 99Driven

File

Chapter 4: Nodes

This chapter gives an overview of what nodes do, and outlines the different types of nodes. It explains the choice of type of node, and processes of starting a node system, creating nodes and flexibly managing them.

Nodes are the containers for your thinking about the data, places to keep emerging ideas and their links with data. If you code data in NVivo, nodes are where coding is stored and explored.

Documents and nodes are symmetrical in NVivo. You can explore and browse both, and you move between the systems by coding and linking.

Overview:

- A node is a place in your project where you can keep ideas and coding. Your project can have any number of nodes;

- Nodes can be used for storing ideas, with or without coding. A node can represent a category or abstract concept, and store its definition, memos about it or links to other nodes;

- Nodes can contain any amount of coding of documents. When you code, you store at a node the *references to the text* to be coded there;

- There are many ways of creating nodes in NVivo, designed to fit into the many processes you are likely to be undertaking when you want a node. Nodes can be created *during coding* or *without any coding*;

- Nodes are managed via the Node Explorer and can be flexibly altered, organized, combined or shifted, created and deleted. Their Properties (name, description and owner) can be changed at any stage;

- Nodes can be kept free of organization (Free Nodes) or managed in hierarchies of categories and subcategories (Trees). Case Nodes can be used to identify all material on cases, and to group them in types that share the same attributes;

- Managing nodes in hierarchical Trees is optional; use it for access to them and viewing of them as a catalog or system;

- Nodes can be managed in any number of Sets for easy access, coding or scoping searches;

- Any node can have any number of DocLinks to documents. Any of these documents can be a Memo, which is a full-status document;

* Nodes can be given values of any number of Attributes;

* The text that is coded at a node (including all rich text and links in the original document) can be browsed, viewed in context, the coding spread, and the text recoded in the interactive Node Browser. From the Node Browser you can jump to, or browse, the contents of the original document or any DataLink in the coded text.

Go to the *Reference Manual*, Chapter 4, for instructions on creating, changing and using nodes and the Node Explorer and Browser. Go to Chapter 7 in this book and the Reference Manual for discussion on coding, and Chapter 8 in both books for shaping nodes in sets and trees.

Nodes in NVivo

Qualitative projects need containers for ideas, and links between those ideas and particular data. The task of understanding rich data is always partly a task of abstracting from it. In all varieties of qualitative methods (and much of life), we seek categories that make sense of the diversity of data. Categorizing is a way to "think up" from the data to greater generality. But to do so, of course, risks oversimplification. Qualitative researchers usually seek a balance between being swamped in complexity and being stranded by pre-emptive reduction of data.

Abstraction, categorization and coding

One solution is to identify and bring together the data passages that seem to belong at a category. This is usually called coding, and almost all qualitative methods code (though the techniques and purposes of coding vary greatly). The previous chapter discussed one form of coding, termed visual coding. This is the simplest way of "marking up" text, so everything on a topic can be recognised by color, font, etc. *(See Chapter 3)*

A goal of coding, however, is usually retrieval of all the data coded at a category. Visual coding only serves this purpose for very small projects. Researchers need a method not only of finding all coded passages, but also of returning, if necessary, to the context in the original record. Other goals are much more challenging; the researcher may aim, for example, to explore all the retrieved data in context, to develop new, finer categories and gain new understanding, combining and linking categories into webs of theory.

If you have worked with paper records previously, you may have used folders or index cards (even shoe-boxes) for housing categories and storing copies of, or references to, the appropriate data. Each topic or theme which mattered for your project, or was discovered in the data, had a place in such a storage system. In a study of images of scientific research, you might know in advance you will need categories for each of the several research areas in the project sample. You would set up a place for each of these categories, and usually structure it into a catalogue or node system, the folders to be grouped in larger more general categories. As material comes in, you might discover in the data a recurring theme about "trust" of science. Now that also needs a place where you can store ideas about it, and where you can put references to the places in your data where you find that topic or theme. When you want to write about trust, pull out that folder.

Qualitative analysis is often very dependent on such storage systems. Crucial requirements are the ability of the researcher to manage the categories and the task of coding, and the ability to go back to the coded data and retrieve those segments. But that's not usually enough. We are asking not what have we coded at "trust" but how and where trust of science develops, and what situations seem to support it? The crucial challenge is that the categories must be able to support more than just a description of all the data coded there. Why do some people trust science, others doubt? We need to ask questions like "What's the relationship between trust of science and a person's attitude to education?" And then questions like "What do the higher educated people say about trust of science if they talk about preference for natural remedies?" Such questions are almost impossible to ask in shoe-boxes.

In NVivo, categories and the results of coding data are placed not in a folder or on an index card, but in a node. Nodes are the ways of storing ideas and the coding of documents. Nodes are also a central way of asking questions, finding out about any combination of categories or exploring their relationship to other nodes, to particular attributes, or to results of searches. And nodes can be used to filter or scope inquiry, so, for example, a set is restricted to documents coded by a node, or a search to text not coded there.

Nodes are thus quite unlike shoe-boxes and index cards in that they support subtle questioning and cumulative inquiry. You can usually ask and answer a question if you have, or can create, the nodes and/or attributes in terms in which you can frame the question.

Nodes are also the result of questioning. NVivo will give you your answer as a node or nodes, holding the results of searches. Now you can ask another question: "I have a lot of material from educated people who trust natural medicine but also trust science – let's see if they have a romantic image of science."

Thus nodes are the tools you use to perform many processes. NVivo creates an environment in which you can make, manage and explore ideas and categories. The node system supports both creativity and efficiency.

Nodes and other project processes

Nodes and documents are handled symmetrically in NVivo. The Explorers and Browsers offer similar information and access. That symmetry assists development of project structures and helps you get used to the tools for handling data and ideas. Each of the following chapters concerns nodes:

- Nodes, like documents, can have attributes *(See Chapter 5, Attributes)*;

- Nodes, like documents, can be linked. DocLinks can be placed at any node, taking you to any number of documents which can optionally be Memos. Any number of nodes can be linked via NodeLinks. *(See Chapter 6.)*

- Coding of documents at nodes can be done in many ways, and is used to bring together all material on a topic or category to rethink and alter the interpretation. When you browse a node, you can recode and rethink the text that has been coded at that node. The Node Browser is thus a very important locus for analysis. Coding at nodes, and functions of the Node Browser, are discussed in *Chapter 7*;

- Nodes and documents can be managed in Sets. Nodes may optionally be managed in Trees. Sets and Trees provide complementary ways of shaping data *(see Chapter 8)*;

- Nodes, documents and attributes can be shown in Models and accessed directly from the Modeler *(see Chapter 9)*;

- Nodes are how you ask many qualitative questions about the intertwining of themes, or the occurrences of patterns. Nodes (along with documents and attributes) provide the ways of expressing questions. Node and document sets can be combined to scope Searches. When you perform a search, NVivo can save the answer as a node. This means that the material returned by your search is not just text, but coding, and using that coding, you can explore what you found or ask other questions. You can usually ask and answer a question if you have, or can create, the nodes in the node system in terms of which you can frame the question, *(see Chapter 10, Searching)*.

Node Areas

When you make a node, place it in one of three areas:

- Free Nodes (unorganized, for emergent ideas, or unstructured projects);

- Tree Nodes (hierarchically ordered to assist in managing a growing vocabulary of concepts);

- Case Nodes (to bring together all the material about a case).

You can use any or all of these areas of nodes, and introduce them to the project at any time.

Nodes appear in the Node Explorer (see below) in these areas. Any node can also be in two further areas: Recently Used Nodes and Sets. In both these areas, NVivo places an alias (or shortcut) to the node.

Free Nodes

Free Nodes are nodes created without any shape to a node system. This is helpful for:

- The handful of concepts of a project whose goals and time span are limited;

- Categories being created "up" from the data early in coding, as ideas emerge from data;

- Gathering material you don't understand or wish to think about;

- Concepts that do not seem to belong anywhere in your more organized system. These are often the most interesting or puzzling, and it is important not to lose them, because there is no logical place for them. You do not have to organize nodes in a tree structure if you prefer not to.

Tree Nodes

NVivo does not require, but does offer the option of, organizing some or all of the nodes you create in "Trees" of categories, sub-categories etc. Trees of nodes offer management and access, rather as the library node system does, helping you to clarify your concepts, locate a category rapidly, recognize its place in the whole system and see relations between it and its subcategories.

Hierarchical node systems, in "Trees" of categories and subcategories may be constructed at any stage, as a shape is found for the nodes you are creating. Tree nodes are also used by NVivo as an efficient way of storing output from the software's processes. Tree nodes are created by the system for Extracts from documents *(Chapter 6)* and default nodes for Searches *(Chapter10)*.

Case Nodes

Case nodes provide a way of gathering and using all material to do with a case, and keeping together all cases of a particular type. NVivo handles cases explicitly at nodes, and manages case nodes with some rules differently from those at other nodes.

Some studies require the ability to gather and assess everything about a case and to restrict searches to all the cases of a given type etc. This is usually so when individuals, sites or settings are the focus of the research question.

Creating Nodes

Qualitative researchers usually create categories in two different ways: "up" from the data, as meanings of the data are noted and stored, and "down" from prior ideas, project designs and theories.

There are many ways of creating nodes in NVivo, designed to fit into the many processes you are likely to be undertaking when you want a node. You specify its location and title.

Node creation may happen as a focused act or as a side-effect of other acts, e.g. coding. NVivo is designed so that when you need to store an idea, the option to create a node is accessible.

You need do no prior designing if this does not suit your method. For many projects, nodes just happen as a result of reflecting on data.

Creating a node while adding during coding

Many researchers create nodes "data-driven", the category coming "up" from the data. Any of the ways of adding coding are ways of creating a node, since for most qualitative researchers at least some categories "emerge" from data, *(see Chapter 7, Coding).*

You can create a node while adding coding from:

- The Document or Node Browser's Speed Coding Bar - type a new node title into the node Title Box and you make a Free Node, or locate a node in a tree;

- The Document or Node Browser's Coder - type a new node title (and location) into the Find box, and if the node is not found it will be created.

Creating a node without doing any coding at it

Nodes need not have coding. You might want nodes to store ideas, with Memos about them, or to record the category you are curious about but yet have no data to code at. You might also create nodes to represent cases you are yet to study. You can create nodes in many ways without coding at them.

- From the NVivo main menu bar you can rapidly create nodes you know you will want, by selecting the type of node you wish to create and enter the node titles very rapidly, (Type and press Enter.) If creating nodes in the tree, locate them by selecting or typing in the numerical "address";

- Whilst viewing your nodes in the Node Explorer, you can create a node at any place where it is needed.

When you wish to create a node you normally need to specify:

- Where it goes – Free, Tree or Case? If it's a Tree Node, you decide where to attach it in the tree system (i.e. what its address will be). If it's a Case Node, you tell NVivo which is the case type for this node;

- The title of the node. If text has been highlighted and an In-Vivo node requested, the title is the first 36 characters of the highlighted text. Otherwise you must enter the title, (max. 36 characters and different from all other nodes of its class or sibling nodes for tree, case, case-type nodes). NVivo will give a default title in some cases.

Creating nodes to link to an Extract

You can create a node at any time to take you directly to some coded content. You may want to create a cross reference or a citation for some text in your document, or for your node. NVivo calls this an Extract.

Suppose, for example, you are browsing a newspaper article on the recent doings of a senator, and you have in your project the speeches of that senator. When the article refers to a passage in a speech, you would, in the world of paper documents, write a marginal annotation on the newspaper article, possibly scribbling a juicy quote or a comment on that speech. In NVivo, you can hyperlink the passage of your online newspaper article directly to the speech passage in your transcript of the speech.

You do this using a NodeLink *(see Chapter 6)*, to a new node, coding whatever passage or passages in the senator's speech documents you want.

Creating nodes automatically

Under some circumstances, nodes are created by NVivo. Nodes created for you are exactly like nodes you create. You can shift them around, browse and code at them just as you can with any other node.

NVivo will create nodes and code at them if you ask for autocoding of sections. Section coding is a very quick way to make a node for each question in an interview, each speaker in a group, or each topic in fieldnotes - and to automate the coding. *See Chapter 7 in this book and the Reference Manual.*

NVivo will create a node and code at it if you select a Scope and save as a node. If you request this, it will also code the result of a Search procedure. You can choose where it goes by asking to Customize Results and specifying a destination node by title (and location). If this node does not already exist, it will be created in the specified location; *(see Chapter 10, Searching).*

NVivo will also create nodes when you import node attributes. If the nodes do not exist, they are created, *(see Chapter 5)* .

> *Since nodes can have attributes, Attribute Import can be a very efficient way to create nodes! For example, if in an interview project there are to be a number of cases considered, and your first meetings with the people involved produce questionnaire data about demographic details or attitude scales, you may first define the cases in a statistics package. Attribute Import will tell NVivo what the statistics package "knows" about each case – and create the case nodes for you to code in NVivo, the forthcoming qualitative data from each.*

Managing Nodes

Qualitative research is not suited to rigid containers. In NVivo, the nodes and the node systems that contain them are highly flexible. The titles, positions and definitions of nodes, the memos about them and references to documents at them, can be changed as your data and your understanding of it, changes. The node system can be redesigned during the life of a project to express emerging ideas and theories.

Using the Node Explorer

All nodes created by you or by NVivo are displayed in the Node Explorer, with many ways of viewing and managing nodes. It's well worth the time to get familiar with what you can see and do. Even simple use of the Node Explorer offers several ways of viewing, assessing and reflecting on your node system.

The left pane, in the style of Windows Explorer, shows the Node system, divided into recently used, Free Nodes, Trees, Cases and Sets. These expand to show the nodes in them on the right hand side. For any selected node, you can see how much coding it has, the node definition and whether it has children or a Memo.

The number in brackets, beside the area title, tells how many nodes are in that area. It is worth playing with these. Recently Used Nodes will give access to the nodes you have been working with; this may be the fastest way to select nodes. Clicking on the area title (e.g. Free Nodes or Trees) brings you to the list of all nodes in that area. Clicking on Trees takes you to the nodes containing the "top" categories, the "roots" of all the Trees. If a node has subcategories, a plus (+) symbol appears to the left of its title; if it has no subcategories, a minus (-) symbol appears.

Making Sets of nodes

It is very easy to make sets of nodes. You might wish to have all the nodes on a particular problem area in a set so you can systematically explore it. Or all the nodes created since you went on holidays (and took a different viewpoint on the project). Or all those cases that have to do with the fight in the Boardroom. Or ones you seem not to be coding at.

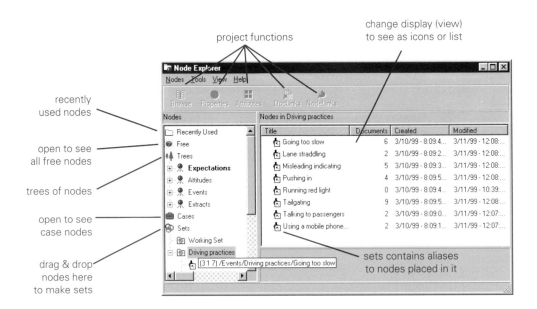

Drag a node to the Sets icon to start a new set with an alias to it, or drag and drop into an existing set. Create and build up Sets of nodes this way to see nodes in useful groupings. Use them for temporary tasks ("This week is Nodes") or for major shaping of contents ("Issues about Trust"). Copy and Paste can also add node aliases to sets. The uses of sets, in managing nodes and accessing them in analysis, are described in *Chapter 8, Sets*.

Going elsewhere from the Explorer

The Node Explorer, like the Document Explorer, has buttons on the toolbar that show you the variety of functions and possibilities for analysis that come with any node. Icons take you to Browse, Properties, Report, Attributes, DocLinks and NodeLinks. Select a node and call it in a Node Browser to browse, reflect on the text and do coding *(see Chapter 7)*. View and change a node's Properties - edit its name, number or description (see below). Make a Report on a selected node or set of nodes *(see Chapter 11)*. Open an Attribute Explorer on the node selected so you can view or change the values of attributes *(see Chapter 5)*. Place a DocLink (optionally making the document linked here a Memo) or a NodeLink at the node *(see Chapter 6)*.

Nodes and their properties

The properties of a node (its number, title and definition) can be changed at any time. A node must have a title and location.

Node title

Node titles are usually chosen by the user. Choosing and editing the title is important to express the meaning of the node. You can choose the title in two ways:

* In the text displayed in a Document or Node Browser, select the characters which will be the title of a new node, and click In-Vivo. This makes a node with that title, coding just those characters. You can select and code a wider context if you wish, *(see Chapter 7)*;

* When creating a node from the menubar, context menu (right mouse click) or whilst coding, type in the title.

> *The title can be any string of up to 36 characters, except the characters used as delimiters, that is the slash '/', colon ':', period '.' and parentheses '( )'. (If these delimiter characters occur in the title of a node they will be replaced with a tilda '~' in the node title.)*
>
> *When selecting text for an In-Vivo node title, you can alter the text in the edit box on the Speed Coding bar before making the node. This is quicker than changing its title to remove any of the delimiter characters.*

NVivo titles the nodes it makes as a result of analysis processes:

* If you wish to place a NodeLink in a document to take you to an extract from another document, NVivo will make an Extract Node and title it "[name of the document] – Extract" *(see Chapter 6)*;

* If you request that the results of a search be kept as a node or nodes, NVivo will title those nodes *(See Chapter 10)*.

Node number

Every node has a numerical address. Changing the number changes the location of a node. This can be important as the relationship of categories is established and explored.

Node description

A description, while optional, is useful for expanding on titles, for recording current thinking on a concept, or instructions about how the node is being used. For example, the node "/People/family", might have a description clarifying the use of the node: "includes all members of own or spouse's family". Many researchers don't bother to describe categories. But you may find it useful to do so:

- Descriptions are a good place to record the use of a category for monitoring over time or in a team;

- You can list nodes with descriptions, providing a codebook. Edit the report of that list for a memo to team members on meanings of nodes. A useful technique for auditing the development of your project is to make a report, with a date attached, and store such lists;

- Keeping dated lists of nodes with descriptions at different stages of a project, or keeping in the memo a record (dated) of changes in descriptions, helps monitor developing ideas, documenting your account of the development of the theory. This may be very important in justifying your processes of analysis and making claims for the validity of your conclusions. If you are keeping an audit document in NVivo, changing node descriptions can be recorded there.

Changing Nodes

Whether prepared in advance or not, a node system will almost always become a problem if it becomes rigid.

It is improved by regular monitoring and pruning of unused or duplicate categories, clarifying vaguely defined ones and shifting and reorganizing trees as understanding grows. The ability to create a flexible node system is critical for creative analysis.

If you change your node system as your ideas change it will provide a clear window onto your project. If this isn't done, the node system becomes a cage for the ideas coming from your data.

Nodes can be created for tentative ideas, to store a question you don't have time to answer tonight, or to explore fine-grained distinctions prior to merging them in a confident category. When the question is asked, or the category confirmed, the node is shifted or deleted.

Nodes rarely stay the same for long, since they express growing understanding of the data. You shift them to represent the growing shape of your analysis. They acquire links and coding as ideas change. You can reflect this by changing from the Node Explorer (at any time):

- The node's Properties;

- The node's location in the node system;

- The DataLinks to and from the node.

- The coding at the node by any means of coding. Each of these changes alters the Project DataBase;

- If you make a Report on a node, this can be edited for printing out for discussion or cutting extracts to paste in a paper etc. *without changing the project*.

Changing Nodes by Drag and Drop

The Node Explorer supports rapid restructuring of nodes, within or outside Trees.

Drag and drop a single node or a sub-tree for reshaping your node system, for instance, bring a series of Free Nodes on related categories together in the tree structure.

Changing Nodes by Cut-Copy/Paste

When you cut or copy a node, it and its coding are placed on a Clipboard. As in a word processor, it can then be pasted as often as you wish and will not be deleted from the Clipboard until something else is placed there. You can view the contents of the Clipboard from the Tools menu on the NVivo menubar.

When you paste a node at another place in the tree, it (with its child nodes if any) is relocated there with the same specific title and number, but the new hierarchical title and address appropriate to the location you chose. Coding at the node(s) and memos will be preserved and the memo will record the fact that this node was cut from elsewhere and attached, to help you log the processes of your project.

Merging Nodes

You can merge coding at two nodes in NVivo. When you cut or copy a node, its coding can be merged with coding of another node, to combine them.

Coding will be merged seamlessly, so the recipient node does not contain duplicate coding. You will be asked if you wish to merge links and if you wish to transfer the attributes of the node to the Clipboard.

Merging nodes is a most useful way of bringing together coding from like categories. Its uses include:

- Building a "bigger picture" as you become more confident of the meanings in the data;

- Building up nodes and coding, to create more general categories in order to recode into new particular ones. Chapter 7 describes ways of using the Node Browser to recode the larger categories to specific subcategories;

- Gathering data coded at categories that have not proved useful, to read and check that you aren't missing something;

- Asking "bigger" questions. For example you might wish to merge all the nodes to do with opposition to an innovation, then Assay that node to find who's at all opposed. Note: it may not be easy to "Un-Merge". To merge coding if you do not wish to delete the node whose coding is merged, or you are unsure that the merge will have the results you seek, select it and merge with the recipient node. If you do not wish to lose the specific coding of the second node, make a copy of that node to receive the merged coding. Browse the results before you do the process permanently.

Note N4 also optionally merges memos at the nodes (appends one to the other). NVivo allows any number of links to documents at a node (any of which may be flagged as memos), as well as links from nodes to other nodes (some of which may be Extracts). These links are not automatically merged. You have the choice of losing those links, merging the contents of the linked items or selecting some links to be NodeLinks at the new node.

Managing coding: the Node Browser

The Node Browser gives you "live" access to browse all the data coded at a node. When you code, references to the text segments you select are stored at the node. When you ask to Browse the node, NVivo retrieves the text on the screen.

Note the symmetry of the Node Browser and Document Browser. In both you can read and code text, and from both you can go to properties and links. Editing of text in a document can of course can only be done in the Document Browser, but you can get there swiftly from any coded text in the Node Browser.

In the Node Browser, you can read the text coded at that node, *view, and optionally code, context* and change the coding directly. This is done by selecting the text you want and coding or removing coding, just as though you were in a document.

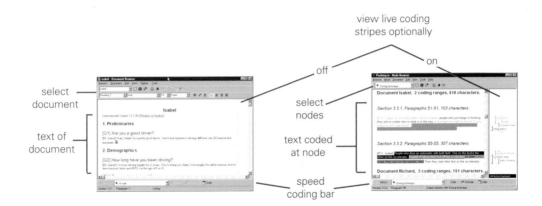

The Node Browser in NVivo is designed for viewing and reviewing that data, with unique facilities for:

+ Rethinking coding;

+ Rethinking the nodes that you are coding at;

+ Changing the coding at the node *in the project*, by adding or deleting references to text units;

+ Combining these processes with all other processes involved in coding and reflecting on coding; making new nodes, reshaping the node system and adding links and memos.

The working of the Node Browser is described in the context of coding in Chapter 7.

Designing your node system

NVivo does not need you ever to create any nodes, and does not care whether you organize them, if you do. They need never be reorganized or shifted. You can also wait until ideas take shape and then organize them. However, organization is a useful way of exploring and expressing the relationships of the categories nodes represent.

If you are unsure about the best way to handle nodes, good advice is to keep track of the categories being created by carefully naming and describing them. Allow organization of them to develop, maybe in Sets, along with the understanding of the data. Management of nodes happens as some categories obviously "go" with others. By moving the uncoordinated nodes into connected groups, you start to get a sense of a *system* of categories, rather than just a mess. By exploring and searching this node system, you see the state of the project, the range and relationships of ideas generated by data, the nature of prior theory, the amount of data collected in each area under investigation, and the need for new directions of data collection.

Ways of organizing nodes

NVivo offers several ways to organize nodes:

- Giving nodes the values of attributes allows you to organize and access them by what you know about what they represent, rather than their logical relationship *(see Chapter 5)*;

- Linking nodes to other nodes, or to the same document, can express a wide range of relationships. These can be as vague as "all these cases had something to say on this problem", or as specific as "this memo links to every node where text about the problem is coded" *(See Chapter 6)*;

- Placing the aliases to nodes in *sets* allows them to "belong" in several places, and the items in sets can have any – or no! – logical relationship. Placing them in hierarchical (category/subcategory) Trees expresses different sorts of relationships *(see Chapter 8)*;

- Placing nodes in a model allows you to draw and link any relationship that makes sense to your understanding of the data. *For more discussion of the choices for managing nodes see Chapter 11.*

Researchers do not need to organize nodes at all. But usually they will! As projects develop, most users explore data and express ideas by coding and storing reflections in nodes; in most methods this requires organization. Nodes in NVivo, probably more than any other aspect of a project, will reflect the researcher's method and the stage of the research.

Organizing nodes in Trees

You can organize nodes hierarchically in Trees at any stage, and for a wide range of purposes. Most commonly, Free Nodes are used for nodes that do not have a clear logical relationship with other nodes, trees for those that do. *Chapter 8 offers detailed advice for using and designing trees of nodes.*

How big should the node system be?

"How many nodes do I need?" is a common question – and one that nobody else should answer for you! The size of your node system will depend on your method. And it will change with your project.

It is usually important to find a balance between a node system too sparse to do justice to the data and one so large it is unwieldy and not used consistently, with the coding task becoming onerous.

A project that aims for a thematic summary of the material, without very detailed interrogation of data, might have a small node system, with a node for each major theme. By contrast, a project whose goals include interpretation which is finely detailed, pursuit of multiple meanings in data, or pattern seeking and validation, will need a much larger node system. Multiple meanings of data are always best handled by multiple coding in NVivo, since the search processes allow fine specification of which patterns of meanings are to be located.

The size of the node system will depend upon whether you wish to code text in fine detail. NVivo does not require, but does have, tools to exploit multiple coding of text. If a passage is about many subjects it can be coded very swiftly at many nodes, so you can use the search tools to explore the richness of your data. This will mean that any rich passage will be coded at many nodes, and you will have a node for each of its meanings.

For researchers who require a lot of nodes NVivo has various ways of managing them to give access to the node wanted, and to allow you to find and review all the categories created. A common problem to avoid, however, is allowing unnecessary growth of the node system. This usually happens when a node has been made for every possible code, and the node management tools are not being used. (Researchers had the same problem before computers, when they stored categories on paper files or index cards. Without computers there were fewer ways of managing the categories.)

For these reasons, whilst NVivo permits a node system of any size, it provides a toolkit for paring, pruning and condensing the node system, to make it as efficient and elegant as possible. You need not decide to do this at the start of the project. You can alter, delete, shift or combine any nodes at any time.

Case nodes and handling cases

Case Nodes are the one type of node for which prior decision is advisable, because they provide special advantages for some projects.

Which projects need case nodes?

No Project requires Case Nodes. Projects will benefit from case nodes if:

- The researcher wishes to identify everything about a case; and

- This is not done through the document structure.

Case nodes are *not* needed for the two following types of projects:

- Some projects do not require that the researcher be able to study and compare cases. Perhaps the goal is to study a process of development of a community, or the multiple meanings of a treatment, but there is no interest in understanding how the process is differently experienced by different residents, or the meanings for different categories of patients. Such projects do not need case nodes. (Such projects could be seen as single-case studies: the *community*, or the *treatment*, is the case for study);

- In some projects the data is structured in such a way that documents concern one, and only one, case. Perhaps each resident was interviewed alone and only once, and no resident discusses any other one. Or each patient's account takes just one document. (In these projects, the document represents the case, and there is no need for a way of narrowing or broadening enquiry. The document from this interview represents just what we know about this case, and everything we know.)

Many projects, however, don't come in such tidy structures. The residents are interviewed several times and turn up in meetings you have observed; moreover, they constantly talk about each other! The researcher needs a way of keeping track of everything to do with a particular resident.

Coding at a node for the case is the most efficient way of doing this. Code at the node the whole document if it is an interview with her, and just the characters of text where she speaks in the group, or someone else talks about her.

NVivo will further assist by ensuring that all cases of a particular Case Type can be accessed together. So you can have nodes for all cases of residents separate from nodes for all cases of nonresident activists.

What's special about case nodes?

You can create Case Nodes at any stage in a project (just like any other node), but if you are handling data in Cases, the sooner this decision is made, the better.

Case Nodes appear in a special area of the tree and are different from other tree nodes in two ways:

* They can be organized in types of cases, so you can be reminded which cases belong there, and can view and review the representations of your cases;

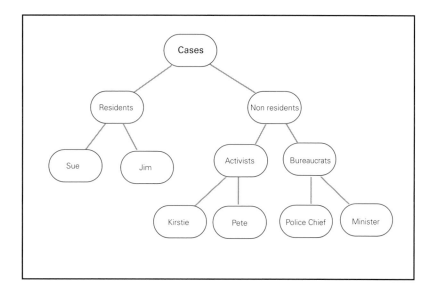

* Case Types can be used to handle the values of attributes consistently. If a Case Type node is given the value of an attribute, then all the Case Nodes under it inherit this value. This saves work and ensures consistency: in the project described above, for example, the Case Type node "Residents" could be given the values of attributes residents will have in common, for example geographic location and role and perhaps socioeconomic status (if you subsequently find a resident whose socioeconomic status is anomalous, you can change the value of that attribute for this resident, (*see Chapter 5*);

* Case Nodes can't have subnodes ("child" nodes). This ensures that each case is a separate item. In the residents' project, you might have case type nodes for all residents and all nonresidents. Sue and Jim are residents so they have Case Nodes under the Residents Case Type node. But the Case Node Sue can't have a subnode for Sue's work experience or Sue's political values – since these are not cases of residents.

> *Why keep coding of the case separate from coding at other categories? When your program supports sophisticated searching, multiple meanings of data are best handled by multiple coding; this is a good example of the power of such coding. If you have a node for work experience, and code everything on anyone's work experience at that node, you can ask questions about how work experience relates, for example, to activism. If the text also concerned the experience of a person for whom you had a case node, you would also code that text at the case node. Now you can ask about everything to do with that case, and also compare different cases about the effects of work experience on urban activism.*

What can you do with Case Nodes?

A Case Node can be used for simple retrieval or for more subtle shaping of analysis by filtering Sets or Scoping searches *(See Chapters 8 and 10)*. If everything about each case is coded at a case node you can do the following:

◆ Simple retrieval of coding taking you to just the data required when you are writing a case study of this resident *(see Chapter 7)*;

◆ Filter Sets of documents or nodes according to whether they contain material on this case or case type *(see Chapter 8)*;

◆ Scoping searches that support comparison of cases, comparing for example her contribution to the development process with another resident's. Scoping searches by combinations of case nodes and attributes allows comparing the contributions of all *female* residents with all *male* residents *(see Chapter 10)*;

Most projects that consider cases concern more than one type of case. For example, the urban study might concern cases of residents and of nonresident activists and nonresident bureaucrats. If you have separate Case Type nodes for these cases, you can efficiently assign values of attributes and also part data powerfully for analysis, for example:

◆ Retrieval by Case Type node takes you to all the material from one type;

◆ Scoping a search allows comparing values of residents and nonresidents to a particular issue;

◆ Scoping searches by combinations of the case nodes and attributes allows comparing the contributions of all residents who had moved in before a certain date with those of later arrivals and nonresident activists.

> If you have used nodes to identify all the material on a case in a NUD*IST4 project, these will be imported into NVivo as ordinary Tree nodes. You could of course relocate them as case nodes in NVivo, but there is no need to do so unless you see the special handling of attributes and Case Types as an advantage at this stage in your project.

Profiles and Reports of Nodes

Nodes, like documents, can be reported on out of NVivo, with a wide range of report output options, including counts of items and coding, and displays of coding. These are fully outlined in the *Reference Manual*.

You can display (and print) profiles of nodes (like documents). A profile is a table of data whose content you specify. It might be a table of all the nodes in a set, profiled by the values of a particular attribute. (All cases of the case type "teacher" by "years of experience" or by coding at nodes "attitudes to continuous assessment".) Use profiles for rapid viewing of the range of your data, for careful assessment of a sample's representativeness and for exporting to statistics packages or any other table-handling program, such as spreadsheets, for displaying the results of searches.

You can print any report from NVivo; text coded at a node will appear in rich text. Print the Browser displays of documents or node contents, with their coding stripes and numbered paragraphs and sections. Save or print the contents of (text coded at) nodes in rich text, with all links identified in endnotes. Create comprehensive rich-text Reports to list information on all areas of your project for editing in NVivo, saving or printing.

This chapter gives an overview of attributes and their values, explaining the different value types of attributes and suggesting how you might choose between them to tailor them to their intended use. It discusses the design of an attribute system to store information about the project's documents and the people, sites etc. represented by nodes.

The attributes system makes information storage easy, and more economical with space than using base data coding. Attributes won't appear in the index system, so conceptual categories will be uncluttered by information storage nodes. There is no limit to the number of attributes and values.

Overview

♦ NVivo allows you to store any number of attributes for documents or nodes respectively. Each attribute can have any number of values;

♦ By specifying attribute values for documents or nodes, you can store information that applies to the whole document, or text coded by a node, representing any data in which you are interested;

♦ NVivo is designed to make information storage as easy and as automated as possible. Attributes and their values are swiftly created, altered and allocated;

♦ Attribute values can be numbers, strings of characters, Boolean (true/false) or dates and times. A document or node can have only one value for each attribute;

♦ Simple tools are provided for viewing and altering attributes and assigning values to documents or nodes as they are introduced to the project, or more is learned about them;

♦ All attributes are given the three null values 'Unassigned', 'Unknown' and 'Not Applicable', allowing researchers to specify the appropriate reason why no other given value (a value that you define for an attribute) has been assigned, and to use this knowledge to make analyses more rigorous;

♦ Project consistency is maintained. All documents have the same attributes (although different values may be assigned for each attribute). All nodes have the same attributes. Documents and nodes may (and usually will) have different attributes. But if a given attribute is defined for both documents and nodes, it will have the same values in both systems. NVivo checks new attribute names to ensure consistency;

♦ You can import attributes of documents or nodes from a statistics package or other table software. NVivo will create the attributes, values and documents or nodes if they don't exist;

♦ All analysis processes can include questions or restrictions to do with the values of attributes of documents and nodes. These include the filtering of Sets by attributes *(see Chapter 8)* and Scoping and Assaying searches *(see Chapter 10)*;

♦ You can export any selection of attributes for any selection of documents or nodes, or a table for import to a statistics package or other table software.

The *Reference Manual*, Chapter 5, contains instructions for creating, changing and exploring Attributes and Values. Remember to use help files at any dialog or window when you need more information.

The role of attributes in qualitative projects

Qualitative research is usually less about factual information than about discovery and interpretation of meanings. Most researchers wish to store *information about* documents or people, sites, events, and other phenomena. Such storage of information is often referred to as descriptive coding. Researchers storing such information can then use it in seeking patterns and asking questions about the project.

The use of such data is often different from its use in surveys. The historical researcher might have a sense that isolation in an early colonial community was entangled with women's marital roles and changed with years of marriage. (The Tutorial Project "Doing Rustic" offers such data.) The diary and letter accounts are complicated, it's hard to see patterns, but by reviewing and rethinking the stories from women in different marital relations and from different class backgrounds, the researcher aims to find the critical issues for each. We want events and accounts to be dated: let's have everything she wrote about isolation after the move from Sydney, or after five years of marriage. The goal is not to prove a statistical relation between years married and isolation, but to thread together the beads of narrative, or to gain an understanding of how marital instability and time passing contributed to the loneliness of making a new home in a new country.

Such information is usually stored in separate records, or accessed by the researcher's memory. NVivo allows it to be stored swiftly in the form of attributes of those documents or people etc. Attributes have different values (for instance the values of the attribute "gender" are "female" and "male"). An item can have only one value of an attribute.

Descriptive coding can, of course, be done at nodes that represent the values of attributes – this is how it is done in NUD*IST4. But this technique has two limitations. Firstly, creating "base data" nodes carrying such information can require a large number of nodes and unwieldy index system. Secondly, representing such information by coding is actually misleading. If we code the document that is a letter from a man at the node for "/gender/male", we have to remember we are indirectly storing information, not about the text, but about the person we know is the speaker.

If you have worked in NUD*IST4 you probably used "base data" nodes for storing such information, a procedure for which N4 has been much praised. Why change it?

♦ Attributes in NVivo do more, in ways that are more efficient and less obtrusive than nodes and coding in N4. This takes the task of descriptive coding, and the nodes it required, out of the index system.

- Documents or nodes can have attributes;

- Attributes with numerical or date values mean you can ask questions in terms of *ranges* of values (everyone over 25) or time periods (after the peace settlement);

- The uses of attributes are integrated through search and analysis processes, offering much more than the ability to restrict to a base data node in N4, or use one in an index search. Hence N4 users are likely to find many more uses for attributes than for base data coding.

  There is of course no reason why nodes should not be used in NVivo as ways of storing information by coding at base data nodes that represent the values of variables. N4 projects imported into NVivo will retain all nodes, including base data nodes. Unless the base data coding is only just begun, you may find it better to continue than to create attributes and values. However, base data coding in N4 can be exported to a table which can, after some editing, be imported to NVivo as attributes and attribute values.

Using attributes in NVivo

Information about a document can be stored by specifying a given value for each document attribute. If it is an interview with a man it can be given the value "interview" of the attribute "data type" and also the value "male" of the attribute "gender".

Qualitative data does not often come tidily parcelled in document sized chunks. People, events and so on are represented in parts of many documents. This is why NVivo also allows you to store any number of attributes for nodes (see below). NVivo ensures consistency between document and node attributes.

The attribute system in NVivo is more economical, with respect to space, than base data coding. It is designed to allow the flexible use of information about documents or the parts of your project represented in nodes.

Project-wide consistency with document and node attributes

As many attributes of documents may not be relevant to nodes (and vice-versa) they are handled separately by NVivo.

However, document and node attributes are linked in such a way that attributes are global in a project. When a document attribute is created with the same name as an existing node attribute (or vice versa), they automatically share the same values and value type. This ensures that the values of an attribute that applies to both documents and nodes are used consistently.

This consistent use of values prevents confusion. For example, you might specify the attribute "Gender" for documents, with the values of "f" and "m" (because some documents are interviews and you wish to store information about the gender of the respondent). If you later decide that "Gender" should be an attribute for case nodes, you will be informed that this attribute exists as a document attribute and already has values allocated. This prevents you from creating different values (e.g. "male" and "female") for the same attribute (otherwise your project could contain four genders!) Now you can investigate women's responses by specifying the attribute value "Gender" is "f" – and that will apply to both documents and nodes.

Using the Attribute Explorers

Each Attribute Explorer offers a multifunction display of all attributes for documents and nodes respectively. It is one of several ways to create and change attributes and is designed to suit the many research processes attributes support *(see below and Reference Manual, Chapter 5)*.

A node can have attributes, just as a document can and the processes of creating and allocating attribute values are entirely symmetrical, as are the processes of using attributes in analysis.

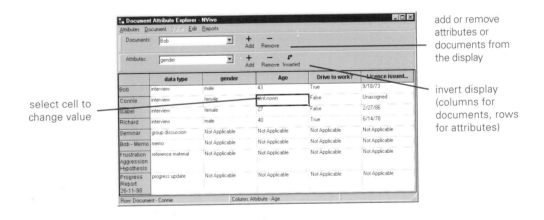

add or remove attributes or documents from the display

select cell to change value

invert display (columns for documents, rows for attributes)

Whether you use the Attribute Explorers to create attributes or not, you will find many other uses for them. If attributes matter for your project, it matters that you should be able to view and review them efficiently. The clear and flexible graphical display allows you to see the values of attributes and alter them swiftly; to view, review, adapt and change the attributes in your project, profile the distribution across a sample or compare the patterns of attributes for a series of documents or nodes. For many projects, the Attribute Explorers take on the sort of multifunction display role of a spreadsheet. (You can export the contents to a spreadsheet too if you wish!)

It is worth spending some time getting familiar with the research uses of all of the Explorer's features. They are designed to allow you to focus on the attributes and items you are interested in. You can add, remove and rearrange items in the display to aid comparison and rename or change attributes, assigning existing values to particular items or creating new ones.

Using document attributes

Any document (including, of course, Proxy documents) can be given any value of a document attribute. Document attributes are appropriate for descriptive coding that applies properly to a whole document or documents. They might record the following features:

- The origin of the document (e.g. data about the interviewer, history of creation);

- Relevant dates for the document (e.g. date a message is sent or an observation conducted);

- Document-wide features concerned with the content or sources of the content (e.g. data about the author, what it's about);

- If a person or site is represented by the whole document, attributes might store information about them (e.g. demographics).

An interview project has three team members doing face to face interviews, whose transcripts create a document for each person interviewed. Analysis will require access to considerable demographic details of respondents, comparison of team interviewing styles and examination of changes in the project over time. Document attributes include 'interviewer' (a value for each team member), 'date interviewed' (day/month/year) and demographic variables 'gender' ('female'/'male') and 'age' (number recorded). Values for each document can be entered directly or stored in a table and imported automatically.

Using node attributes

Like documents, nodes can also have attributes and attribute values. The processes of creating and allocating node attribute values are entirely symmetrical with those for documents, as are the processes of using node attributes in analysis.

It is easy to see why documents have attributes whereas the need for node attributes is less obvious. However, node attributes are helpful in most projects since the data that you want to store information about is rarely represented by a whole document or documents. A major innovation in NVivo is that nodes can also have attributes.

A focus group transcript contains speeches by many people, yet you want to store the values of attributes like 'gender' and 'age' for each of them. One school site is represented in many documents and parts of documents, but you want to store its attributes of 'location' and 'staffing level'. How do you record the attributes of that person or site wherever it is represented?

For many projects, this sort of information is best assigned to a node, (e.g. for a site or a case) which can code many parts of different documents. If each participant in a project has a case node, for example, you can give that *node* the appropriate value of the attribute gender. If case node Steve is assigned the attribute value gender=male then NVivo "knows" that everything coded at that node was contributed by a male.

Every time you code with that node, the coded text also acquires the attribute value gender=male. Now any search or enquiry can include restrictions or questions about the attributes. In this way, the information is "piggybacked" on the coding.

Examples of this use of node attributes might be:

♦ Information about a site or setting;

♦ Information about people discussed in several documents.

Other uses of node attributes refer to the node itself, for example:

♦ Date at which the node was created;

♦ Information about research team members. Each member has a node, which codes all the memos they have written, or perhaps all the interviews they conducted.

Case Node attributes (a special use of node Attributes)

Cases is a special area of nodes in NVivo that assists researchers whose analysis requires gathering and exploring all the material (from parts of a document or documents) on a case *(see Chapter 4)* .

A Case Node can inherit attribute values from its Case Type Node. This assists the management of cases since there may often be several types of cases. You decide which attribute values are given to Case Type Nodes - and the case nodes inherit those values.

The inheritance of values is not merely a convenience: it alerts you to the patterns of data you are creating.

To return to the study of residents and non residents diagrammed in Chapter 4, individual participants were given a case node each; those cases were grouped under case type nodes, which can be given the values of attributes as appropriate.

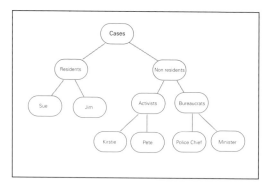

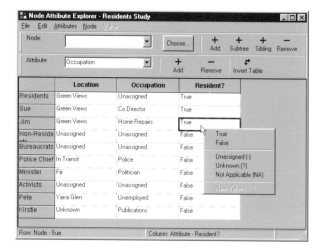

Searching and Scoping searches according to attributes

All analysis processes can include questions or restrictions to do with the attributes of documents or nodes.

One way to do this is via the creation of sets. You can use filters in the Set Editors to create a set of documents or nodes that have the attribute values you specify *(see Chapter 8).*

Filters allow you to specify that items should have a value "less than", "equal to", "not equal to" or "greater than" a particular value. Thus you can ask questions about happenings before the outbreak of war or use several ranges of values to ask questions about men aged between 20 and 25, between 50 and 55 and over 70, all at the same time.

A set created in this way can be used to restrict your search to documents or nodes having these attribute values. This process is known as Scoping of Searches. *(See Chapter 10)*.

The ability to store attribute values of documents or nodes is unique to NVivo. If you have not hitherto attempted systematic storage of information in qualitative projects, it is worth reviewing the ways in which attributes might be used to manage data with respect to the requirements of your own projects, the uses of attributes in scoping and doing searches, and the uses of case nodes in managing attributes.

For example, if all of the schools studied for a project are in the same district and socioeconomic area, they can be specified by assigning values for district and socioeconomic area to their Case Type Node 'Schools'. If you wish to use different attribute values for each case (for example a high class religious school is located in a lower class area) then assign the value 'Unassigned' to the Case Type Node and any of the existing attribute values (or new ones) to each Case Node.

	District	Socio-economic
Schools	Richmond	Unassigned
Richmond High	Richmond	Middle class
St Mary's	Richmond	High class

right mouse click any cell to see all current values of the attribute, or make a new value

Low class
Middle class
High class

Unassigned (-)
Unknown (?)
Not Applicable (NA)

New Value...

The information required about each school (teaching level, staffing, facilities etc.) the staff members (years of experience, attitudes to unions etc.) and the students (grade, subjects etc.) decide the Node Attributes, and for each case, the values of the attributes are entered.

Analysis can now ask questions about the data, drawing on this information (for example, give me all the accounts from high-graded students at low staff level schools about their long-experienced staff members and compare with the attitudes of low-graded students in the same schools).

Attribute values

Values of attributes can be strings of characters, numbers, Boolean (true/false) or dates (ten different forms are provided).

> *Some attributes obviously come in only one of these forms, but researchers often have a choice. For example, it seems obvious that the attribute "age" requires numeric values, especially since NVivo will allow the exact numeric age to be specified (even to decimal points). But sufficient information might be carried by values of "youth", "middle age" and "old age" in a project where specificity of age group does not matter. On the other hand, an attribute for "Self-assessed Age" could have more subtle meanings and be given string values to represent these in a project about the meanings of aging. The values, created as different perceptions of age are discovered in the data might be "painfully young", "mature", "just old enough to be independent", "young at heart" and so on.*

Your choice of value type should be informed by what you want to do with the attribute. Some salient features of NVivo's handling of values may assist your choice.

Strings of characters

An attribute can have any number of different string values with names you type in, limited only by the limit of the number of characters that will fit in the box (which of course depends on the characters typed, since letters take different spaces.) For those who like such facts, you can fit in 19 "w" characters or 79 "I" characters! However, you will find it helpful to keep value names as short as possible, since they can be viewed more easily in the on-screen table display.

Some string attributes may have values that possess an intuitive order but are not arranged in the same order alphabetically. An attribute "Temperature" with values (in alphabetical order) "cold", "cool", "hot" "normal" and "tepid" could be more usefully defined as "1cold", "2cool", "3normal", "4tepid" and "5hot".

Numbers

An attribute can have any number of different numerical values.

One significant advantage of numerical attributes in NVivo is that you can specify exact values rather than having to resort to a few ranges of values (for example "Age" = "25-30", "30-35" etc.) Using attributes this way, you can avoid reducing the detail of what you know about, for example, income or age group or the number of members of a group. Make an exact value for every item, then in analysis you can Scope searches, exploring the relevant groupings of values. Does life really begin at 40? Ask first, "What do people aged 40 or under think of their lives?" and then change the Scope to ask, "what of those 40 to 45?"

Boolean

The values "True" or "False" are the appropriate values for many attributes – for example "Ever Married?" or "Had Vasectomy?". These are the sorts of attributes for which even the most reality doubting researcher will usually accept a true/false answer.

However, it is advisable to consider the data reduction in using Boolean values for qualitative questions. Researchers often do not know in advance the meanings they will discover in rich data. The significance of a particular historical period, or an especially vulnerable age group may emerge from the data during the project. Check what you can do with numerical or date values before you decide to use Boolean values.

Dates and times

The provision for dates and times as attributes is new in NVivo and designed for projects with interest in process, history or chronology.

Date/time attributes are of particular importance for nodes. Qualitative data is always examined in its context and "time" is always a significant aspect of context. Most qualitative projects contain process – the history of an organization, the memories of an interviewee, the events of a life history, the dates of significant transitions in a family history, or more immediately, the timing of entry into the field and significant moments in observations. If your project requires that your material be examined in the context of time, you can do this by using date/time attributes for nodes. A node for each stage or event can be dated, and the Search procedures allow you to scope searches by date/time and retrieve by date/time.

When you create a date/time attribute you choose the largest and smallest field out of year, month, day, hour, minute, second. So date/time attributes can be used on very different time scales – differentiating years in world history or seconds in a transcript of a contentious focus group!

Using Date/time attributes for analyzing time

You can of course code data manually or on computers at event dates, with category titles like "11 August 1940" or "12:30 pm". But time in qualitative research is usually about process, not events. What NVivo offers with date attributes is different because it allows filtering of sets and searches according to ranges of dates and times, so you can specify all dates earlier than a chosen one, or everything that happened before this time.

Suppose you have several documents in which eyewitnesses describe drug trafficking transactions, such as making a deal, handing over the goods and paying for them; you create nodes for coding descriptions of such events. Then create a node attribute, say "When?", to record the times of these events. If one deal happened on 8 March 1999, give its node "Deal-1" the "When?" value of 8 March 1999. Do this for the other event nodes (perhaps keeping those nodes in an "Event" tree). Now NVivo's search facilities can easily locate the events (nodes) happening after a particular deal, or before a particular sale, or payments made at the same time.

Date/time attributes in years can give access to large spans of history, or you can date down to the second if you're studying fast interactions (maybe you have documents with many video or audio clips in them you need to time-stamp). If its weekly patterns you're studying, you can even deal with weekdays and times within them.

Since nodes and documents can have many attributes, you can give a particular node many dates or times for different aspects of what it describes. You could have "Start" and "Finish" attributes, you could have "Dominance Established" and "Agreement Reached" attributes for your ten nodes coding ten committee meetings you studied. Then NVivo can be asked if agreement was ever reached in any meetings before someone established dominance, or indeed which ones never had dominance established. If you're trying to reconcile several eyewitnesses, you might have attributes "Katy Date" and "Bob Date" to handle their different dating of the same events. You can then show these attributes for the events (nodes) that interest you, using the tabular layout of the attribute Explorer, and rearrange and explore to reveal the patterns you seek. Or use the Modeler to lay out the time series of the trafficking transactions.

As part of project management, which NVivo is designed to handle internally, you can give your interview documents date attributes such as "Interview Date", "Transcription Date", "First Coding Date", and anything else that helps to organize your project.

No need to restrict values

There is no restriction on the number of values an attribute may have. There is, of course, efficiency in selecting from a smaller number as you assign values to a new document or node. But NVivo is designed to avoid the need to reduce values preemptively, especially in the case of numerical and date attributes.

Remember, analysis tools in will allow specifications of less than, equal to and greater than a numeric value. This is important since qualitative researchers often do not know when they start which ranges will matter in later analysis. So if it suits, give the exact age or number of children, etc. or the exact date, preserving the uniqueness of each item. Searches can be restricted e.g. to "over 40" or "before 1994".

Handling the absence of information

NVivo provides three null values (their abbreviations appear in parentheses) 'Unassigned' (.), 'Unknown' (?) and 'Not Applicable' (NA).

These give different reasons for absence of information. Many documents or nodes will have no assigned value for an attribute though it does apply to that item. A different situation is when the information is not known – and it is important for the user to record this. Different again is the situation in which no value is assigned because this attribute doesn't apply to the item (the Project document has no gender, etc.).

A document or node receives the attributes currently defined for all documents or nodes respectively. Any or all of these may have a default value. The system default is unassigned.

Designing an attribute system

You will get most from the attributes system if you see it as highly flexible. Few projects begin and end with the same fixed list of things they are interested in.

For each attribute that you know you will need, NVivo asks you to provide a name, a value type and the default value. Each of these can be used to design a system that works well for your project.

Name

When you name an attribute, select a name that is specific, so you will not become confused. Note the names are case dependent.

NVivo will check no other attribute in the project (document or node attribute) has the name, and also that it is not the name used for an item's property, e.g. "Description" or "Title". If the name is in use, you will not be able to create a new attribute with the same name. Note you can create, name (and later delete) attributes for any research purpose. Try one called "coded thoroughly?" with boolean values. Now you can exclude from rigorous searches any document not yet coded thoroughly!

Value type

Choose one of String, Number, Boolean or Date-Time (see above). The default value type is String.

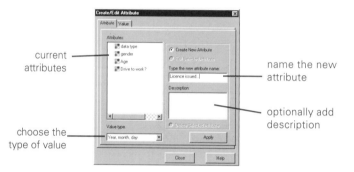

current attributes

choose the type of value

name the new attribute

optionally add description

Default value

Whenever you create an attribute (and at any later time) you can specify what the default value will be (Not Assigned is the system default). This reflects information about your current knowledge of the data and the relevance of a particular attribute value. If most of your research participants are women, set the default value of attribute "Gender" to "Female". When a new item is introduced for a male, simply overwrite the default value. It is useful to be systematic in using these values (see below).

Starting an attribute system

Of course, a project does not have to use attributes at all, but most researchers will find them highly useful. In starting your attribute system, keep in mind that all analysis processes can include questions or restrictions to do with the attributes of documents or nodes.

The best way to begin is to set up attributes for:

♦ Things you know you know about people, sites, and other items in your project. For example, most interview projects know they will have basic demographic information about respondents (gender, age and so on) and will have that information immediately available when an interview is done. Set up the attributes so you can assign the values as each document comes in;

♦ Things you know you will want to ask about and find out about. For example, you may not yet know the levels of training attained by the teachers at the schools you will study, but you may know this is an area of importance in the project. Thus you will need a node attribute "level of training". Having it there will remind you to find out about it.

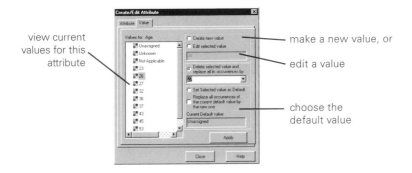

view current values for this attribute

make a new value, or

edit a value

choose the default value

Creating and editing attributes and values

You create an attribute and its values through efficient processes accessible from the (Document and Node) Explorers and Browsers. They can be typed in rapidly or selected, in either the Create/Edit Attribute window or the Attribute Explorers, with full tabular display of the attributes and values for documents or nodes as you instruct. Full instructions are included in the *Reference Manual, Chapter 5.*

A list of initial values can be created for each attribute before they are assigned to any items (school grades "1", "2", "3", "4", "5", "6"). These are easy to type in and can be changed at any time. For example, you might start with the values "Rural" and "Urban" for the attribute 'Location', then when you realize the significance of semi-urban locations and different rural settings you might add further values and assign them to items that are considered to suit those values. (Note the similarity between this process and coding-on from a node representing a broad category!)

You may also want to delete an attribute value or replace all of its occurrences with a new or existing value. Both the Attribute Explorers and the Create/Edit attribute tool allow you to do this. To give a document or node the attributes of some conceptually related node, you can copy the attributes of another item.

At any time you can alter or delete an Attribute, change the type or specifications of its values or alter the values assigned to an item.

Importing and exporting a table of attributes & values

You can create attributes and values, and assign values to documents and nodes by importing a table. The importation of an attribute table will create documents, nodes and attributes not already in the project. The attributes' value types are also defined in the import table.

Document	Data Type	Gender	Age	Drive to Work?	Licence issued
Bob	interview	male	43	true	9/18/73
Connie	interview	female	Unassigned	false	Unknown
Isabel	interview	female	27	false	2/27/86
Richard	interview	male	40	true	6/14/78
Seminar	group discussion	Not Applicable	Not Applicable	Not Applicable	Not Applicable

You create the table in any software that makes tables (statistics package, spreadsheet, word processor etc.) Save it as tab-separated text and import to NVivo. *(See Reference Manual Chapter 12 and Appendix A as well as the online help for detailed instructions.)*

This table can be used for creating only attributes by omitting the details of documents, nodes and values. Create the table if you know in advance what attributes this project needs, import it and they are set up. Now simply add the values when they are required for incoming data.

> *For some projects, importing attribute tables into an empty project is a very efficient way of setting it up. Table import will populate the project with documents and/or nodes and/or attributes of a value type specified. It will allocate a value to each document or node thereby creating value lists for each attribute. This is most useful in a relatively structured project, where the shape of data is known in advance.*

To export attributes for documents or nodes, select the attributes and items you want in the Attribute Explorer. Make a report, selecting the tab-separated format. *See Chapter 11 for a discussion of linking with statistical data.*

6

Of the ways for connecting data and ideas in NVivo, the most direct and immediate are DataLinks. Earlier chapters have indicated the range of links you can make between your documents, ideas, and other data. Documents can become compound, by linking them to other documents and nodes in the project, and to internal annotations or external files. Nodes can be linked to other nodes or to documents reflecting on ideas they code. This chapter is about the methods of making and using those links.

Overview

◆ NVivo supports three new types of qualitative DataLinks, each designed to allow the researcher to review linked items, or go elsewhere. Each allows two different uses:

1. DataBites link a selection of text to a text bite stored internally or to any external file. This means you can from that point:

   Write or edit a text annotation or

   Open and run external files, of any sort that your computer can run - text, picture, audio, video, or any readable file.

2. DocLinks link a document, a node or a place in the text to any number of other documents. These documents can optionally be memos, and can be used to:

   Link to any existing Project document or documents,

   Link to a new Memo document.

3. NodeLinks link a document, a node or a place in the text to any number of other nodes, and thus to data coded there (and from there, if you wish, to the source document). These can be used to:

   Link to any existing node or nodes:

   Link to a new Extract Node, coding just the extract you want.

◆ Links that take you from the top level of a document or node are symmetrical, pairing data items. You can create, access and remove them from either of the linked items. Links of any of the three types that take you from a place in the text (in-text links) can be created, accessed or removed from that place in the text.

- ◆ If you code a passage that contains a DataLink, the link will be coded with the surrounding text. It will appear and be live in the Node Browser, so you can access the items linked when you view coded text;

- ◆ There is no limit to the number of hyperlinks between documents, or from documents to nodes.

Go to the *Reference Manual*, Chapter 6 for how-to instructions on making and managing each of these types of links, and for handling the multimedia files that can be linked to compound documents

Qualitative linking and compound documents

Every method of doing qualitative research requires many ways of linking. Coding is one way. The act of coding links the selected passage of text to the category created for coding. When you code data in NVivo, you make links between nodes, the data they code and the context. NVivo offers unprecedented support for qualitative coding, with a range of ways of selecting text, coding, viewing that coding and jumping to context or related coding *(Chapter 7)*.

But *as well as* coding data, usually *before* coding, or sometimes *instead* of coding, researchers wish to make direct data links.

In manual or computer data handling there is usually a strong emphasis on coding because linking is supported *only* by coding. However, qualitative research requires other ways of linking – *out* of the project to other material, and also *within* the project to other documents and ideas, linking document to document, document to idea or linking directly to a particular extract. Most of this is given little support by computer (or other) methods of handling data. Researchers have had to rely on their own ability to "see" and remember links. Qualitative research often involves linking that is done prior to coding, or that is not possible by coding.

NVivo is designed to support such qualitative linking. In doing so it introduces an entirely new way of thinking of data. If you have not read Chapter 3, you might like to review its discussion of compound documents. If you have not read Chapter 4, check it for how nodes work.

> *As you review the options for linking, think of them as options for constructing compound documents. The ability to edit and grow documents, linking them to sources outside and inside the project, is central to the goal of bringing data alive. Rather than work with "original" data from which "interpretation" is derived, a researcher can accrue insights and discoveries, draw comparisons and build theories in documents that grow as understanding grows.*
>
> *It is also useful to think of DataLinks as providing new ways of seeing and using nodes. Nodes hold references to coded data. But they are not rigid containers, and never the end of a methodological path. If a link takes you to a node, the node can take you to the documents coded there, or to ways of asking questions about them.*

This chapter is about these new ways of linking. A major focus of the development of NVivo was on ways to integrate coding with *qualitative* ways of linking. Like the hyperlinks now familiar in web browsers and advanced word processors, these links take researchers somewhere else. But they are specifically designed to be managed, so the researcher is not left in "hyperspace". DocLinks and NodeLinks are symmetrical. From the linked document or node, or from the ones linked to, you can review, change and add to the links you have made.

Making DataLinks

All three types of DataLinks can hold links to more than one item. There is no limit to how many links you can place at a document, a node or within the text of a document.

These new ways of linking data are simple to use and easy to manage. In each case, NVivo walks you through the necessary steps to locate which data you wish to access through that DataLink.

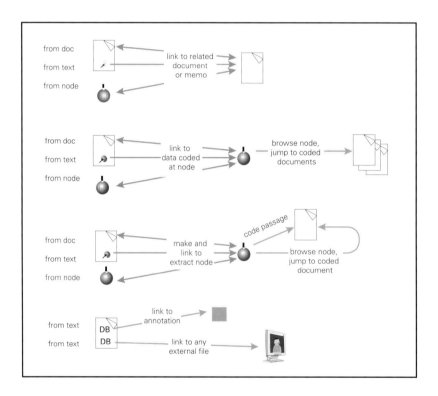

DataLinks anchored to documents or nodes as a whole

DocLinks and NodeLinks (but not DataBites) can be "anchored" at documents or nodes as a whole. You can link a document or node to any number of documents and nodes.

When whole documents or nodes are linked to other documents and nodes, the link provides access in both directions. For example, if an interview document is linked to a Memo about the respondent and to the respondent's second interview then you will find that the Memo is linked, in turn, to both interview documents. In-text DocLinks, NodeLinks and DataBites in the text point to a document, but it is not linked back to that text spot.

DataLink anchors

All three types of DataLinks can be "anchored" by special symbols in the text where you specify the link. These indicators are designed to facilitate management.

♦ DataBite anchors are passages of text you select: they have special underlining and coloring (green). You may wish to mark the words that are commented on (for example a passage of discourse you wish to annotate) or insert (in text) a description of the file accessed by the DataBite (for example "tape records laughter at his revelation").

♦ DocLink and NodeLink anchors are represented by their respective icons (see above) and appear at the point where your cursor was when you inserted the link. Each anchor can hold links to as many documents or nodes as you wish.

All DataLink anchors stay "live" when you code them. When you browse that text in a node, or when it is part of the retrieval from a search, the anchor is displayed. In the Node Browser the link will call the appropriate annotation, external file, document or node, just as if you were in the Document Browser.

If you copy and paste text from a Document Browser into another NVivo document, the DataLinks will copy and be "live". (Of course, if you copy and paste text from a Browser into a document in another application, e.g. a word processor, that application will not be able to activate NVivo's links. Hence, DataLink icons will not be copied into the new application.)

Choosing what you link to

When you place the link, you specify the link, and NVivo takes you where you need to go to define links:

♦ If it's a DataBite to an annotation, you are taken to an edit box; if to an external file, you are taken to the file selection box. Choose a file – any file! (but check first if your computer can run it!)

♦ If it's a DocLink or NodeLink, you are taken to the relevant window to select the document(s) or node(s) you wish to link.

You can return to an anchor at any time, and alter or add to the items linked there.

DataLinks anchored to documents or nodes, as a whole, can be used in conjunction with in-text DataLinks. This provides quick and easy access to related items within your project memos.

DataBites: linking to annotations and external files

DataBites can be placed anywhere within an NVivo document. Any document that is imported, created in NVivo, or created as a Proxy can have DataBites, transforming it into a compound document.

It's worth reflecting on the sorts of data your project will manage and the ways each of them could use these links to other places. The two different sorts of DataBites (Annotations and external files) answer different needs:

DataBites are intended to mark small passages of text with their special color and underlining, not very large passages, and one DataBite won't be accepted across paragraphs. (If you insert a paragraph marker in a DataBite it will lose the "severed" section after the paragraph mark.) If you want a DataBite to apply over several paragraphs, use the ability to color or change font to mark the relevant section (and edit in a note to that effect).

> *DataBites will be particularly important in building documents that hold together the often messy and at first disconnected data and preliminary interpretations in qualitative projects. See discussion in Chapter 11, "Bringing it Together", on Project documents and Audit documents.*

Annotations

Qualitative researchers working in their data often need to jot notes, record thoughts and hunches or remind themselves of other sources of evidence or images related to the document. DataBites are for making such links by embedding "bites" of other sorts of data in your document.

These can be internal annotations. They are accessible from the DataBite anchor (which can be pre-existing text or text you type in to identify the annotation) and can be printed out in reports as endnotes.

An Annotation is like a stick-on note, a plain text file attached to the document at a certain place, but not a document in itself. Unlike DocLinks, annotations do not take you to a normal NVivo document (The normal document would be in rich text, codable and able to take DocLinks and NodeLinks). The annotation stays there, can be altered at any time, will appear in coded data and can be output as an endnote in reports.

Examples of uses of annotation DataBites are:

  ◆ Interpretive comments in text finely analyzed for discourse patterns;

  ◆ Translations of passages in another language;

  ◆ Researcher's notes on body language or movement during the transcribed interview.

External files

Researchers whose documents refer to other files often need immediate access to the original for illustration, evidence or vivid recall. DataBites can embed any other file in the document – jump to the DataBite and NVivo will call the application and open that file.

DataBites to external files are intended to take you elsewhere. Researchers are often swamped by large monomedia sources; an entire report or a complete video of hours of action can be very unhelpful. The DataBite allows you to access a smaller extract of the report or the video, selected and saved as a small file for this purpose in the context of your summary or partial transcript. (If an external file is very substantial, it is probably best represented in a Proxy document. There it can be summarized, and accessed accurately via coding.)

Examples of use of external file DataBites (each of which would call different applications) are:

 * In a focus group transcript, audio clips from parts of the tape that were important change points;

 * Video segments vividly illustrating the situation described in observation notes;

 * Relevant web page addresses;

 * Word processor files of papers interpreting this event.

You are not restricted in the size of files called by DataBites. The external file can be any file elsewhere on your computer, of any size, for example word processor or spreadsheet documents, pictures in bitmaps, sound and video clips. So long as you have the application to run it, when selected via the DataBite it will run. You can change the external file as you wish.

Usually, however, these will be best used for small bites.

DocLinks: linking to a project document

Links to other documents can be made from a document, node or from anywhere in the text of a document. The DocLinks window, called from the Document (or Node) Explorer and Browser, shows all the linked documents.

To make, view and review links you go to the DocLinks window, choosing whether to link documents to a place in the text or to the document as a whole.

In the DocLinks window you can:

*   Add or remove documents linked at that in-text anchor, document or node. Note that removing a document from the Documents Linked box does not delete the document, just the link;

*   Jump to a selected document in its Browser;

*   Link a new memo. A Document Browser opens on a new document, provisionally titled with the name of the document or node followed by "– Memo" (to differentiate it from that document). You can change its name and Memo status using Properties.

You can use DocLinks to weave together data records and reflections:

*   The link could take you to any document that offers further material for interpretation. For example, in field notes of observations in public meetings, you might place DocLinks where particular people are mentioned, and link the notes to individual interviews with the participants after the event;

*   The document might have a DocLink to the literature review you wrote on public associations and their functions in suburban situations;

*   In your memo on the role of public associations in overcoming isolation in this housing estate, you might place DocLinks to each interview where women talked of their experiences in public meetings;

*   An Audit Document or Project Document *(see Chapter 3)* might become an amalgam of DocLinks as you describe the ways you developed your understanding of the estate.

> *If you use DocLinks in records of the project history, consider archiving early memos (keep them in a set) using DocLinks to the earliest records of your observations or interviews. The current versions of those memos will develop differently as you edit and link them, but the early versions record the origins of your theories.*

Linking to documents that are not Memos

To maximize benefit from DocLinks in NVivo, explore the uses of links to documents that are not Memos. Compound documents can be built up and woven together by thoughtful placing of links to relevant other project documents.

Any document might contain a reflection on, or refer to, or contain discussion about any other document, or any part of a document, or about any node. Qualitative data is like that! For example:

◆ People interviewed talk about others you have interviewed;

◆ In a subsequent group discussion people contradict what they said in
their individual interview;

◆ Your field notes on a meeting throw light on an interviewee's account of
that meeting;

◆ Your data contradicts an argument in the literature review.

In any such situation you can insert a link to the related document (and, if
you wish, edit in text or insert an annotation, commenting on the reasons for
the link). In NVivo, linking operates independently of a document's Memo
status. While many linked documents are obvious candidates for Memo
status (e.g. a document recording theoretical thoughts about the node "career
advancement") it may be inappropriate in some cases. For example, the
document "Sam - first interview" is linked to subsequent interviews with
Sam but you feel it is not appropriate to define any of these documents as a
Memo.

Memos and DocLinks

For many researchers, the most obvious use of DocLinks is to link a
document or a node to memos about that data or that idea. *If you have not
read Chapter 3, you might review the discussion there of memos in NVivo.*

Using DocLinks, ideas can be stored at any point in the data in memos of any
length and any number. For those who work with memos, it is important to
recognize that memos in NVivo are full-status documents. You can edit,
code, define attributes, add other DataLinks and to place memos not only at
a document or a node but anywhere in the text.

Note that just as documents linked by DocLinks do not have to be memos, so
too, memos do not need to be located in relation to other documents by
DocLinks. You decide if it is methodologically useful to distinguish memos
from other data. And you decide which documents should be memos.

NodeLinks: linking to a node, and coded text

NodeLinks take you to the Browser showing all the text coded at a linked node. The idea of a NodeLink is entirely new in NVivo, and a radical way of bringing together linking and coding.

Most researchers are familiar with the ability to jump to documents in web browsers or word processors.

Jumping to browse a node has other functions. The Node Browser shows all the text coded at that category and allows you to jump from *there* to the original document or to spread to view a wider context. It allows you to code and change coding at other nodes and jump in turn to them.

Insert a NodeLink anchor at a document or node, or at any place in a document (imported or proxy) by clicking on the NodeLink icon on the Browser bar or selecting NodeLink from the menubar.

Selecting NodeLinks or clicking on the anchor will take you directly to the Node Browser for that node.

To view and review links, you go to the NodeLinks window. This opens when you select NodeLinks from a menu or when you right mouse click on a NodeLinks anchor.

In the NodeLinks window you can:

♦ Add or remove nodes linked at that anchor point. Note that removing a node from the Nodes Linked box does not delete the node, just the link;

♦ Jump to a selected node in its Browser;

♦ Make a new Extract Node coding a particular passage or passages of your data, (see below).

Using NodeLinks

You can use NodeLinks to blend data and interpretation in many ways:

♦ The link could take you to any node or nodes coding all the material on a particular theme for comparison. For example, if a document is an interview in which one woman discusses the advantages of distance education, then it might carry at that point, a link to the node at which you have coded the few other discussions of advantages, so you can jump to these and compare;

♦ The document might have a NodeLink to the case node for this woman. The link would take you to everything you have coded about the case in question, so you could explore reasons why she might see the situation differently from others;

◆ In your memo on advantages of distance, you might place NodeLinks to each case where women talked about both advantages and disadvantages;

◆ An Audit Document or Project Document *(See Chapter 11)* might become an amalgam of NodeLinks as you describe the ways the concepts were developed and the growing interpretation of the material.

> *If you use NodeLinks in records of the project history, a powerful technique is to keep an archive area in your index system. Store copies of early versions of nodes, linking to these to show how the concept first developed, or was understood at the early stages of the project, then linking to the current node to show how it changed as the material built up and was rethought.*

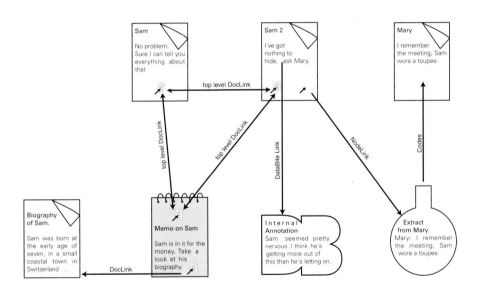

Extracts and NodeLinks

Often the qualitative analysis process identifies passages or quotations the researcher wants to jump to directly. Sometimes the requirement is to find the exact words that were used somewhere else – somewhere outside this document. Sometimes the researcher simply wants to retrieve that text. But more often, once there, the qualitative researcher wants to keep thinking and interpreting.

In NVivo, the ability to link to a node has been extended to enable a direct link to any particular passage, and from there to the context. To do this qualitative task, the researcher needs a special sort of hyperlink. Extract Nodes provide the answer.

Perhaps you are coding an interview (with a doctor, about women's health) and recall that in another document (your field notes from a community meeting) the same person gave a contradictory opinion to what you are now hearing. (In that public venue, he had expressed concern about overuse of the hormone treatment that he is now telling you he confidently prescribes). You may want to insert a link in the interview that will display *just that quotation* from your field notes, for later consideration of this difference in views according to context. You need to insert that link whilst the contrast is clear in your mind, and in a way that allows you to recontextualize the contrasting passage in your field notes later on.

What's needed is a hyperlink that does three jobs:

- It acts like a citation to the target data;

- It also, much more usefully, *takes* you to the document cited;

- Thirdly, and most importantly, you need a link not just to the source document (as web browsers offer) but to the exact passage or quotation you want to see. To be taken to the entire text of your field notes (recording that long meeting) is frustrating because when you come back to the link you may not recall the exact passage, so the work of identifying it will have to be redone. At the time of making the link you knew exactly which passage or quotation was relevant. Later on you may not remember, and under pressure, may not have the time to pursue the link. You might even misremember why you created that link in the first place – which issue discussed at the community meeting was relevant here? If you cannot remember, you lose the highly significant passage containing the contradiction.

NVivo addresses this special qualitative research need through a new use of nodes. Since a node contains references to text, if you *browse* a node, you see that text. From there, you can jump to browse the *original*.

An exact passage (or passages) can be linked to an item by creating an Extract node. By using a node for this special task, NVivo offers to the researcher pursuing that link,

- Immediate retrieval of just the relevant segment(s) of the text, including any DataLinks in that retrieved text;

- All the other facilities of the Node Browser, including to jump to the original document, with that segment highlighted, to keep editing and coding and to spread context *(see Chapter 4 and Chapter 7).*

If you link to an Extract of document text, "Make Node (Extract)" in the NodeLink window, NVivo will make a new node. It will then ask you to select the document containing the quotation that you wish to link and open that document in its Browser. You can then select the passage and code it (by any of the means of coding) at the new node.

Note that you can code as many passages as you like at this node and even flick to other documents to cite passages from them as well.

Upon closing the Document Browser you are returned to the place where you started the process.

The new node appears in the Node Explorer in an area of the index tree provided for extract nodes. It is provisionally titled with the name of the document from which you coded the extract – e.g. "Extract from DAVID". It is a full-status node and you can now rename or relocate it and use it for further coding and in analysis processes such as scoping or conducting searches.

- It can be used to continue coding, and it is available through the Explorer displays and the Coder. You can also, of course, delete the node or merge it with other nodes.

- It can be given DataLinks e.g. a memo about this stunning contradiction;

- If you wish, you can continue to use that node – renaming it, changing its description and shifting it to another place in your index system.

Integrating DataLinks

The design of DataLinks in NVivo is intended to facilitate a style of qualitative thinking that researchers report as a central goal. Researchers build their understanding of data cumulatively, recording insights, coding, going to other data records, reflecting on coding, changing memos and revisiting earlier discoveries. Linking techniques in NVivo are integrated with each other and with editing and coding, so that researchers can escape linear patterns of data "collection" and subsequent data "analysis" if they wish.

NVivo is designed so it is not only easy to place DataLinks, but also easy to manage them. You will find it easy to make links and important to review and thoughtfully revise them if the compound documents you are creating are to be navigated easily. Exploiting these ways of expanding documents, the researcher can rapidly lose the sense that "original" data is different in kind and divorced from interpretation.

Please read on! Linking is easily integrated with Memoing, Coding, Shaping, Modeling and Searching.

7

This chapter is about one of many ways qualitative researchers link data to ideas. This is to create categories and place at them references to data. NVivo does this by coding at nodes.

Coding is an important part of any qualitative research and different methods require varying techniques. Different styles of coding express different methodological goals and different relationships of the researcher to their data.

This chapter discusses the different ways of coding at nodes for different methods and at different stages of a project. It advises how to choose the best way for each of your research purposes and how to integrate visual coding, attributes and node coding.

Overview

* NVivo has three ways of connecting data and categories: visual coding, attributes and node coding. They serve different strategic purposes; and can be combined.

* NVivo supports any amount of coding of documents at any number of nodes. Each method has the same result. References to selected characters, specified paragraphs or sections of a specified document are placed at the specified node or nodes;

* Coding can be done by selecting text on-screen in either the Document Browser (viewing and editing the text of a document) or the Node Browser (viewing and exploring the text coded at a Node);

* Any characters of a Document can be selected for coding on the screen. That is, there are no fixed text units for coding references. In-Vivo nodes can be created and named from text selected;

* On-screen coding can be done with either of two tools:

  The Speed coding Bar allows fast and flexible coding and creating of new nodes, selecting from recently used nodes and In-Vivo coding – one-step coding creating nodes, naming and coding them with the text highlighted;

  The Coder combines coding by drag and drop, or typing or finding a node, with viewing of the coding at a node, and ways of changing and managing nodes;

- Coding can be done by nominating what is to be coded, using any of three tools:

  The Paragraph Coder allows selection of nodes and specification of passage, to be coded by paragraph number for rapid coding of external files;

  The Section Coder automates coding by number or text of sections;

  The Search Tool allows coding of a selected scope or a search's results.

- The many ways of coding can be combined in the Document Browser with rich text editing, annotating and other DataLinks. Coding is not done in a different mode from editing. Coding of text remains consistent when text is edited, or when DataLinks are inserted;

- The many ways of coding can be combined in the Node Browser with the ability to spread a retrieval to see and optionally code wider context, and return to the source document. This supports recoding and coding-on to make new nodes;

- All ways of coding are combined with ways of simultaneously viewing the text already coded and the nodes that code it. NVivo provides these through coding stripe displays, highlighting of coded text and listing of nodes coding a selected passage or part of the current document. Coding can be performed while any of these views are displayed.

The *Reference Manual*, Chapter 7, gives full details on use of each of the tools for coding, ways of doing and changing and viewing coding.

Go to the *Reference Manual*, Chapter 11, for how to profile coding of a document or set of documents, or profile the coding at a node or set of nodes, and how to use the profile display and export a profile to tables for import to other software.

Go to the *Reference Manual*, Chapter 12, for importing and exporting of coding.

Qualitative Coding

Coding has many purposes and is done in many ways in qualitative research. Researchers rarely want to do coding and nothing else. The ways they want to code vary with their research data and purposes. If they are forced to code in only one way, and to rely on that way for access to data, coding can become tedious and deadening to new ideas. Major criticisms of software to date are that it forces users to rely (too much) on analysis by code-and-retrieve techniques and that those techniques impose an inability to edit coded text. NVivo does neither.

Much of this book has been about coding. Chapter 3 discusses the uses of rich text capability for marking up and identifying passages – which we termed visual coding. Chapter 4 discusses the qualitative tasks of abstraction and categorization and the ways these can be done by creating nodes to store categories and coding data relating to that category by placing references at the node. You may wish to visit those sections if you have not read the earlier chapters, as the present chapter builds on them.

No simple typology of coding adequately describes the range of purposes it has for qualitative researchers. Many textbooks distinguish two very different sets of purposes: creative and descriptive. In practice, they overlap. In NVivo, you can do both by editing visual effects, or making nodes and coding at them, or you can choose to do descriptive coding by making attributes and specifying the values of the attributes for particular documents or nodes *(see Chapter 5)*.

With the advent of qualitative computing, coding by placing references at the category replaced visual coding, not because researchers lost interest in visual coding, but because computer programs for coding and retrieval required plain text. They also usually required that coded text remain unchanged: NUD*IST4 was new in its ability to edit text without invalidating coding. Given the formidable advantages of coding and retrieval, researchers turned from visual identification to coding by storing references to, and thus retrieving, (plain) text.

NVivo has no such restriction. Traditional methods of visual coding can be performed on a computer by editing text and inserting DataBites. NVivo allows you to combine visual coding with coding at nodes, or to return to more traditional methods, use visual coding instead of node coding. Whether you use rich text editing for visual coding will depend on how you wish to work.

The (many) goals of coding at nodes

The central tasks of much qualitative research are to extract and abstract – to locate significant themes in complex data, consider them together and abstract from them, providing rich descriptions, categories and theories. This involves noting text of importance, differentiating between different threads in data, jotting notes and reflecting on the tiny insights and recognition of themes that are often the beginnings of theory.

Most researchers before qualitative computing, achieved these tasks by "marking up" paper records (or later, editing in word processors) by highlighting, underlining and scribbling in the margin. The most common way of coding was with color. This coding could be a swift and use visual identification of everything on a topic (purple is for problems) or a very careful, complex marking up of overlapping themes (problems in workplace get purple and crimson).

Visual coding on paper had huge advantages. It was fast, and did not interrupt reading and thinking. It was not seen as a separate process from reflection, requiring a separate loop through the data. It did not take up extra storage space. It was visual – glance at a page and you could see its themes or topics. (A lot of purple there!) Above all it did not "decontextualize" – when you returned to that discussion of a problem it was in context.

However, these methods were inadequate for some purposes. Retrieval was tedious; it is easy to color-identify everything about a topic across many documents, but time consuming to go back through those pages looking for all of the purple highlighting. Retrieval was thus more likely to be inadequate; it is much easier to find a juicy purple passage than all the text coded purple! Scribbles in the margin were hard to read and limited by space. But most importantly, visual coding could not support the next step beyond retrieval, to ask another question about the topic.

Manual filing systems, and later, computer coding at categories, solved some of these problems. At the category (node) were stored all the references to text about a topic (e.g. problems in gaining acceptance in this workplace). The computer can retrieve all these references and display the text. As software advanced, it could not only retrieve text but also use those retrievals to ask another question (what did the people who claimed that they had problems in gaining acceptance in this workplace say about previous workplaces?) But this method had two disadvantages. It made coding a separate research process and it meant that questions had to be framed in terms of nodes. With NVivo, this is not the case.

Creative coding: visual or node coding?

Most qualitative researchers use coding to create categories for thinking about their data, linking all the data to be thought about in this context to the category. This is a highly creative process, and whatever method is used, it involves at least two analytical acts:

- The decision that this is a category relevant for thinking about the project;

- The choice of the data segment or passage that "belongs" at this category.

In NVivo, creative coding can be done simply, by using the visual effects of editing (*as described in Chapter 3*).

Why would you code at nodes then? There are two answers.

Firstly, visual coding is of course highly limited. Coding is restricted to the (small) number of categories that can have different visual representations, and multiple coding of any passage taxes the editor's ingenuity. Thus, as recommended in Chapter 3, visual coding is best used for early, tentative thinking about data, indication of a few topics or to differentiate types of data. For example, in the Tutorial Project "Bush Schooling", the researcher edited the email texts being analyzed to show which part was the message being replied to.

Secondly, once the coding is at a node, the node itself is an item for analysis (*see Chapter 4 on nodes and their uses*). This is crucial in qualitative abstraction. The processes of theorizing from data involve making and exploring categories, not merely retrieving bits of text. If a node is created for each category, coding is a first step to other analysis processes, not an end in itself.

- The text coded at that category can be browsed, edited, put in context and linked back to the original text;

- The coding process can be combined with every other way of developing ideas (visual coding, attributes, linking, models and searching);

- Locating the category (in Free Nodes, or relevant locations in the Trees) records its place in your growing understanding, and reflects your judgement that this category is different (perhaps subtly) from others created so far;

- From the node the researcher can code-on to make nodes for finer dimensions of a concept or category;

- Record your concept formation by using the properties of the node to name and record a description of it;

- Memos and links to other documents and nodes make it part of a growing fabric of linked ideas;

- By giving the node a range of attribute values you can record your knowledge of what it represents. Thus it becomes a meaningful concept not merely a container;

- Making a node of the category means you can return to it the context of the data, rethink and re-code the "original" document. The ability to *rethink* coding once you can view and review all the material coded at a category is essential for qualitative theory building.

Many researchers start coding early in a project as a way of thinking "aloud" about the first data, recording hunches and surprises. The categories you create may at first have nothing to do with each other. In NVivo, you can place DocLinks to memos about these tentative ideas or make Free Nodes to store them, moving them into a more organized index system later, if and when their significance becomes apparent.

Alternatively, you may have a lot of prior ideas about the topic from earlier studies. You could locate them at nodes so you can look for the data related to them. They may be usefully organized in an Index Tree. (*For ways and examples of shaping nodes in the tree, see Chapter 8.*)

Descriptive coding: attributes or nodes?

Coding can be used for the clerical task of storing data (just as it is in a survey). This may be information about characteristics of people or sites – often called *demographics* – or information about the data document. Some studies' analyses rely on the ability to explore patterns and themes according to things that are known about the participants, settings etc. Most studies have some such information to store.

In most manual and computer methods of handling data, descriptive coding can be extremely tedious.

As detailed in Chapter 5 the attributes system of NVivo is designed to take such descriptive coding tasks away from the Index system. Using attributes for characteristics of documents or nodes is much more efficient than using coding since:

- The node system can become very large if such information storage is done through coding, since the node system must have a node for each value of each variable;

- The attribute system is designed so that values can be swiftly created, allocated and examined (profiled);

- As outlined in Chapter 5, the attribute system contains functions not available through nodes (Number and Date/time attributes for example).

> Descriptive coding can be done with nodes; the choice is yours. Nodes can be used to represent the values of variables, and variables can efficiently be organized in a Tree. If you have been working previously in NUD*IST you will be familiar with this method of storing descriptive coding. But check first the advantages of attributes.

Combining visual coding, attributes and node coding

Combining visual effects or visual and node coding, you can see connections in ways not possible either on paper or in previous software. Rich text is not made plain by node coding. So visual coding is retained in the Node Browser. Thus you can browse two lots of coding at the same time.

If anything about problems is purple, and all commentary by you is in italic, purple italic text represents your comments on problems discussed. Browse the node "career advancement" and you can see immediately that some text coded there is purple, even if it had not occurred to you to explore the issue of work setting problems in this context.

If your interest is in seeing where the themes overlap (do workplace problems turn up in all discussions of career advancement?), the answer is on the screen. This is another way of seeing patterns. View coding and examine the colored margin lines (coding stripes) in Browsers or Reports to see what *other* nodes the purple patches are coded at.

Thus coding text at "IV Drug Use" you might use a DataBite to insert an annotation about the context: "He wouldn't talk about his IV drug use because his parents were present". If restricted to node coding, you might have coded at nodes "IV Drug Use", "Reluctance to talk", "Case group interview with parents". To find the context of the uninformative interview, you would guess the relevance of parental presence, confirming it by searching the intersection of these nodes.

By using visual coding (either rich text or DataBites), you not only remove this extra step, but you ensure that this context will be shown to you whether or not you think to look for it. When you are puzzling over the text coded at the node "IV Drug Use" you will see the color-coding or the DataBite anchor immediately.

> *Visual coding is visual – only seen when that text is browsed or reported. If you wish to retrieve all the places where text, coded visually, relates to problems or reluctance to talk, do this via node coding. There are several ways to achieve this, the simplest being to code the specially formatted text appropriately at a node. Note that this cannot be done automatically by text search, as searches are not color and font specific. However, to ensure you can code automatically later, insert a unique keyword (e.g. Ppl for purple) whenever you use this color.*

A particular way of using visual coding deserves mention. If you are coding in a broad category (say, "Reluctance to talk") and are aware that you will probably want to code-on into more specific categories when reasons become clearer, use color or font to identify the different sorts or sources of power. When you browse the 'Reluctance to talk' node, these passages will be color-identified – just select and code, from the Node Browser, creating new finer categories as required.

- In a project with a very short deadline, use in-text visual coding first, coloring text and inserting keywords, then subsequently use text search to autocode the in-text editing if they only gave you until next Friday to present your results;

- Insert subheaders - e.g. level 9 subheader – for a comment, and make that comment a paragraph. You can see the subheaders, in the Document Explorer and jump to each place visually coded this way.

	VISUAL CODING	NODE CODING
Aims	* Record first impressions; * Mark material for later consideration; * Highlight significant passages; * Show shapes in data (responses, events etc); * Edit, expand, annotate; * Finely explore textual detail, conversation structure, iterative patterns.	* Create and manage categories; * Add and remove references to text passages relevant to these categories; * View and review coded material; * Return to source to rethink, maybe recode it; * Browse text coded at a category; * Reflect on material coded at a category, "coding on" to make finer distinctions, new categories for dimensions; * View patterns of coding and explore them.

Techniques	Edit text;
	Insert keywords;
	Annotate process represented;
	Change text
	    * colour
	    * font
	    * style.
	Insert DataBite annotations.
		Select text on screen (in Document or Node Browser) and use either
		    * Speed coding bar
		    * or Coder;
		Decide coding on paper or external file and use
		    * Paragraph coder;
		Format document and automate coding with
		    * Section coder.

Ways of coding text in NVivo: select or combine these to suit your purposes

Ways of doing coding at nodes

NVivo provides a wide range of ways of coding at nodes. You can select the methods that feel best for your (different) purposes.

Full instructions for each method are in the *Reference Manual*. Four tools allow you to do coding at nodes. These are:

* The Speed Coding Bar

* The Coder

* The Paragraph Coder

* The Section Coder

* The Search Tool.

Each of these methods of doing coding has the same result; references to specific text in a document, or documents, are stored at a category (node).

The first two tools, the Speed Coding Bar and the Coder, are ways of coding selected text on the screen. You might want to code from the document, or you might want to review and recode the text coded at a node, coding-on to create new categories. Both the Speed Coding Bar and Coder are available in the Document Browser and Node Browser. The Node Browser has special ways of taking you to the context of coded material for reviewing it.

In either Browser, coding references can be finely delineated, down to particular characters, if selected on the screen.

The second two tools, the Paragraph and Section Coders, are ways of doing the coding by nominating document segments and the node they should be coded at. The paragraph can be nominated by number, or the section located by level or text string.

The search tool offers ways of coding at nodes, coding a scope and coding the results of a scope.

Why have different ways of coding?

Most projects can use all five ways of coding, for different purposes:

* You are exploring a document early in the project. You might be "thinking aloud", browsing and editing comments and annotations to the document, asking why a phrase seems out of place, making an In-Vivo code using that phrase, and coding the context. In such an exploratory mode, coding is as much about category discovery and creation as about the allocation of text passages to particular categories. You are likely to want to create nodes "up" out of the data.

In this case, you will be working in the Document Browser and probably using the Speed Coding Bar. You might then go to the Node Browser to rethink that Free Node, and use the Speed Coding Bar there.

- You are exploring the data building up in a mature project and refining your node system. Contrasting with past coding, the patterns in a new document, you gain a sense of which categories seem to be recurring. Reviewing the coding so far, you create finer categories to do justice to your rich data. In this situation, you want to code at existing nodes (and find them fast) as well as making new ones (and placing them carefully in your developing index system). You need to review the results of the coding you have done already, and view what other selections are coded at a particular node.

The Coder allows you to do all this, and you can do it in the Document or Node Browser. You can also use the search tool to search text for words of interest, saving the results as a node.

- You or a colleague are working away from the computer, on printed copies of your documents, marking them up and making decisions about coding and category creation.

Transfer this coding to your project swiftly with the Paragraph Coder. To code whole documents rapidly, make a set of them and use the search tool to code that scope a node.

- Your data is shaped by questions, speakers, topics, and you want to be able to see (immediately!) all the answers to a question, or everything a speaker said. This is not a very qualitative task, so you want this coding done for you.

Format the documents appropriately and the Section Coder will do it in seconds.

Coding with the Speed Coding Bar

Whether you are in a Document Browser or a Node Browser, the Speed Coding Bar is at the bottom of the Browser window. It shows at which node coding will be added or removed.

When there is a Browser selection, the Speed Coding Bar allows you to:

1. Code (or UnCode) at Recently Used Nodes by selecting them from the list in the bar's Node Title box;

2. Code at nodes (Free, Tree or Case nodes) after typing their titles into the Node Title box (create the node if it currently doesn't exist);

3. Create In-Vivo nodes, titled with (up to the first 36 characters of) text you have selected, by pressing 'In-Vivo'. Do you want more context? Select and code it at the same node (already selected);

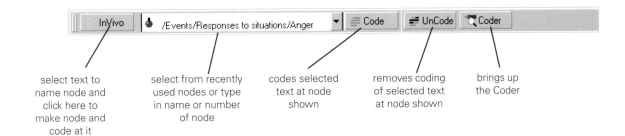

4. Code (or UnCode) at Tree Nodes after typing their address (e.g. '1 1 1') into the Node Title box;

5. Call the Coder. This gives you more control over coding than is available in the Speed Coding Bar.

Note that all the ways of coding with the Speed Coding Bar combine with everything else you can do in the Document or the Node Browser.

- Edit while you code. You will find that the processes of coding can be very different if you are editing at the same time;

- Combine coding with linking, annotating and writing memos as you work;

- The Recently Used Node List allows you to quickly review the way you have been coding;

- Scan another document for related nodes: select it in the Browser's toolbar;

- In the Node Browser, flick between nodes to check whether some of the text coded at an existing node should be coded at the new node. Code context in that Node Browser or jump to the source document to code in the Document Browser.

Coding and Viewing Coding with the Coder

Call the Coder from the Speed Coding Bar or the Browser menus to bring up
the small Coder window. It does a lot of things for its size (and you can
resize the window if you wish).

When there is a Browser selection, the Coder allows you to code in any of the
following ways:

1. Select a node from the Coder's Explorer-style display or List of Nodes
    and press the Coder's Code button;

2. Drag the node onto the text selection to be coded or drag the text
    selection onto the node;

3. In the Coder's type-in box, enter the start of what you think is the node's
    title or number in the Trees, and press Find; the node will be selected in
    the Coder. Then press Code. If there is no exact match, the Coder will
    perform a "wild" match, showing you the nodes whose titles begin with
    the text you typed. Oops! This is how you find you had two nodes with
    the same name in different places!

4. Type in the start of what you think is the node's title and press Tab. The
    title is completed (or if it shares the same few letters as other nodes' titles
    it is completed up to the point where the nodes differ – type in a
    distinguishing letter and press Tab again) and the node is selected in the
    Coder;

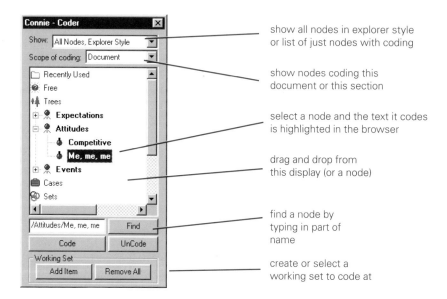

show all nodes in explorer style
or list of just nodes with coding

show nodes coding this
document or this section

select a node and the text it codes
is highlighted in the browser

drag and drop from
this display (or a node)

find a node by
typing in part of
name

create or select a
working set to code at

5. Create or select a set to code at, just like selecting a node. This codes the selected text at all the nodes in the set. Sets can be made rapidly for short term purposes e.g. "The collection of nodes I am always having to code at when I meet this particular argument in various documents" *(see Chapter 9)*;

The Coder can be used in conjunction with the Speed Coding Bar; the latter will display the node you last used to code with whether you clicked Code in the Coder or the Speed Coding Bar. Once you are familiar with the two, you will find that you move between them with ease.

Note that the ways of coding are efficiently combined with ways of seeing the coding you've done:

1. Choose the Explorer-style view to scan all your nodes, select them for coding, rearrange them or move them into sets. Choose the list to view existing coding or to focus on just those nodes being coded at for now. These are ways of reflecting on your data and its meanings, as well as your nodes and their relationships;

2. In the Explorer-style display, use the context (right mouse button) menu for ways of recording your thinking about nodes. Perhaps you realize the meanings of this node have broadened; select Properties and change its Description – and go on coding. Rename the node in the Explorer and go on coding. Select DocLinks and write a memo about your concern that this node now has a very broad application or select NodeLinks and place a link at this node to the related node with a narrower concept – and go on coding;

3. Choose to display nodes that code the document or the selection. These are displayed with bold titles in the Explorer-style display while the List view is restricted to them. You can flick between the two to compare which nodes code the whole document, and which code the text selected – have you forgotten to code at some?

Using the coder to combine coding with viewing what is already coded

♦ What text is coded at that node? Click on a node in the Coder and the text code by that node is highlighted in the Browser. You can alter or expand this coding. If you select text for coding, the highlighting will still show in a different shade!

♦ What else is coded at that Node? Right mouse click at the Node and click Browse. In the Node Browser you have the ability to spread to context or jump to document. To compare it simultaneously with another node in its Browser, use the Browser menu option 'New Browser';

♦ Check out the coding of a related document. Select the other document in the Browser slot (left hand side) and the Coder responds by showing which nodes code this newly selected document. While you are there, note that this is a neat way to check your progress with coding all your documents!

♦ Moving between documents in the Document Browser, check the coding at a node in recent documents (perhaps you suspect your attention wavered). With that node selected, flick back through the documents via the Browser's toolbar, and each in turn will appear with the text coded at that node highlighted. This same tactic will of course allow you to scan quickly the sort of coding at many nodes in specific documents;

♦ While thinking about your nodes and coding in the Coder, you can create and modify sets of nodes using drag and drop (as in the Node Explorer). Perhaps in the coding process you reflected on the thematic relationships of several nodes. Whenever I code at "privacy" I seem to be coding at "home ownership" and "time" – when I get a moment I should explore how these ideas hang together. Make a Set of these and call it Next Week's Work!

Coding with the Paragraph Coder

Your style of research may not require you to code Documents as finely as character by character. It may be sufficient to code paragraphs as wholes; if you're using coding to summarize many customer reports, for example.

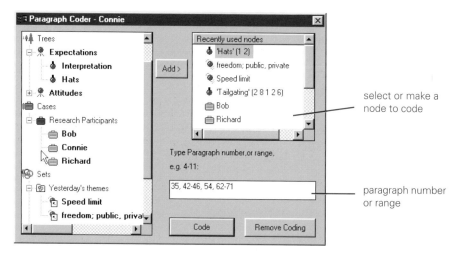

Print out the text of a Report on the Document with paragraph numbers showing. You can now sit under a tree and decide coding. Mark in the margins of your printout the nodes that each paragraph should code. Then later, back at the computer, coding those marginal notes using the Paragraph

Coder will be easy. Call the Paragraph Coder on that Document; as you read the scribbles on your printout, simply type in or select the node to code with, and type in the paragraph numbers it is to code.

Auto-coding with the Section Coder

Coding at nodes can be automated if it is related to document structure or text strings.

Quite often, the documents in qualitative projects have a definite structure. For example, they may be transcripts of a series of structured interviews, all with the same questions in the same order. Or, they may record a series of discussions amongst the same people. In such cases, it is natural, and helpful, to mark sections with the questions (as in the first example) or (in the second example) with the discussant's name when they start talking, like the manuscript of a play. A whole collection of documents may share the same structure, marked by section and subsection headings.

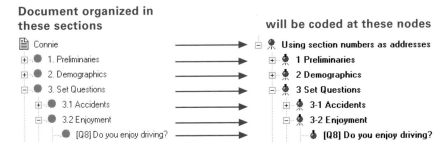

The Section Coder will code all the (sub)sections of a document by their section *heading*, or by their section *numbering* – as tree-nodes with the corresponding addresses. This sort of coding is not meant as a substitute for the thoughtful descriptive coding that only you the researcher can do, but to provide easy access to corresponding parts of different documents. If you have a node for the interviewee Ann, for example, you can use the Section Coder to code by section heading all sections where Ann is the speaker, at a node for "Ann". Or code by section number all sections of the documents where the same question is asked and answered.

To make full use of the Section Coder you have to structure the relevant documents appropriately from the beginning, and that means understanding exactly how the Section Coder works.

Full instructions are in the *Reference Manual, Chapter 7*. Appendix A gives full details on formatting documents for automatic coding.

> In N4, autocoding is done using command files, usually with text search. NVivo does it without command files, either by section coding or through the Search Tool.

Coding with the Search Tool

NVivo will do coding for you in two ways via the Search Tool. Any Scope you specify in the Search Tool can be saved as a node. And any search results can be saved as one or more nodes.

Coding a Scope

The quickest way to get a lot of documents, a set, or the text coded at other nodes coded for you is to use the Search Tool to select that Scope, and save it as a node. If you wish to code a group of whole documents, for example, select them in the Scope pane, and ask to code that Scope at a node. The node is created or the coding merged with an existing node, as you specify.

Coding the results of a search

Results of any search can be coded, so search is a way of autocoding. One of the options in Search Tool is to customize the results by specifying a spread to give context to the finds.

For many projects, the ability to do simple or complex Text Searches is particularly helpful here. The mechanical processes of the computer can locate any string of characters or pattern you specify with wild cards. You have many options in the Search Tool to combine text search with searches of coding or attributes, or restrict the search to just a selected scope. Thus, if words that occur in the text will accurately identify the material to be coded, the coding can be done rapidly and accurately, and spread to the context specified. Use pattern searches, and the options to view finds, to exclude false finds from the search.

But warning: mechanical processes won't interpret. Moreover, whilst coding by text search will do some sorts of coding better than you could do it by reading the text, the computer will certainly make mistakes you would not make. It is very unwise to rely on text search coding unchecked, even for mechanical location tasks (for example, it will miss typographical errors).

A note on coding a proxy document

A Proxy Document appears in a Document Browser exactly as any other Document does, and you can code any text in it by exactly the same methods.

It is worth reflecting on strategies for formatting Proxy Documents in the light of the multiple ways of coding in NVivo.

You can set up your Proxy with numbered paragraphs representing units of the data represented by the document. Edit in your commentary at the corresponding paragraphs. Add DataBites that link to clips from that part of the video.

Code on the screen, using either the Speed Coding Bar or the Coder, highlighting and coding the relevant material.

As for any document, when you view in the Node Browser the text you have coded, DataLinks will be retained live to make this a vivid recreation of the document and your response to it. You may do a very swift job of summarizing and coding a group of videos for example, then a more careful coding through the Node Browser of all the segments on a particular issue. The video clips are available as DataBites, and can be sequentially viewed and further coded as your understanding of the issue develops.

Using the Node Browser

If you are coding at nodes, it is because you want to gain access to all the data that belongs there, for one or another purpose.

You might want no more than to have all that data printed, so you can go away and read it. You might want to copy it into the paper you are writing so you can cite all the juicy quotes on that topic. You might want statistics on what is coded there and you might want to profile the coding and export it to a spreadsheet. All of these aims are achieved by making a report on the node.

However it is most likely, at least at first, that you want this data "live" so you can ask another question, jump back to the source of that quote to rethink it or code-on from this simple category to create more theoretically exciting ones.

NVivo's Node Browser takes you to all the data coded at a node and offers pathways to analysis, rethinking, reporting or returning to the context. The functions and user options for the Node Browser are described in detail in the *Reference Manual,* Chapter 4.

A good working knowledge of the Node Browser is important if you are to get the most from coding. This is not just a retrieval device (though of course it retrieves and allows you to browse all the data coded at a category). Its design reflects the strong theme in qualitative methods that retrieval of coding is never an end in itself. The researcher always wants to go somewhere else from the coded text. Use the icons on the Browser menu bar to select DocLinks to make memos or select NodeLinks to remind yourself of a related Free Node.

Coding-on: using the Node Browser for further coding

The Node Browser is one of the places from which you can *do* coding as well as where you view its results. It is where you can refine and develop your understanding by rethinking categories and coding.

The ability to work "live" in the Browser is essential for qualitative thinking. Researchers can develop ideas by taking this coded data and coding-on into new categories. As in the Document Browser, you can make new nodes as you code. The Explorer-style display in the Coder has all the functions needed to create or shift nodes and to rethink your nodes as you respond to what you are seeing in the recontextualized, coded text.

Using the Node Browser for coding-on is important to much qualitative research. The data gathered at a node offers a new understanding of the category and this often leads to development of new dimensions.

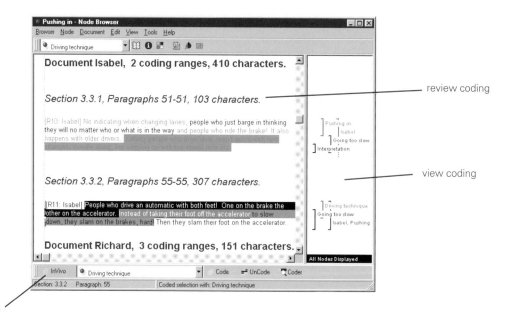

Using Node Browser's presentation of coded material

For each document coded at the displayed node there is a single heading reference which contains the following information: the name of the document, how many distinct passages are coded from that document at this node and the total number of the document's characters coded.

Below each heading reference is a subheading reference for each of the document's distinct passages of coding. They tell you from which section each passage is coded (sections are defined by the heading level formats), which paragraphs (or part thereof) are coded in each passage and how many characters are coded in each passage.

You can choose to show Coding Stripes in the Node Browser to view the *other* nodes at which these passages are coded.

The node browser opens on *all* the coded text but often this can be overwhelming. You can reduce the amount of coded text displayed. Choose whether to see only the headings (describing the passages' source), first line or first and last lines. To scan the sorts of material you have here, select the first line – you'll find the case you were looking for faster, and can then expand to view its context. You will find you select different options for different functions – and that the Node Browser has multiple functions.

Viewing coded material in context

One of the problems of qualitative coding is often the difficulty of "recontextualizing" coded data.

NVivo is designed to make this process immediate. After placing your cursor in the coded passage's heading reference or text you can:

* Jump to the passage in the document (just ask to browse it). Now you can rethink that document, and perhaps edit, annotate or recode it;

* View the context of any passage. Context shown is neither selected nor coded and therefore its appearance is distinct from that of the coded passage. You can select and code some or all of it at the same node or select and code some or all of the coded text and its context at other nodes;

* Spread coding in the Coder environment to code a passage's context. You can spread to a number of characters either side, paragraph or sections. Context or spread functions can apply to all the text in the Node Browser. Just select it all.

Viewing and reviewing coding

Researchers often wish to see what they have coded where, and especially to see the ways that their coding shows patterns in the interpretation of data. You can view coding on the screen or print out visual displays of coding.

Viewing with the Coder

As described above, the Coder allows viewing of the nodes coding a selection or document, and viewing of exactly the text coded at a node.

- View nodes coding a document or selection, by selecting your preference in the Coder selection slot;

- View text coded by a particular node, in either a Document or a Node Browser, by selecting the node in the Coder. All text coded by that node is displayed with a colored background in the Browser contents.

Coding Stripes in the Document or Node Browser

Coding Stripes can be shown beside the text through all editing and coding processes, showing what coding you have already done. They also give a rapid visual trigger to pattern discovery and inquiry.

In either Browser's "View" menu select to "Show Coding Stripes". This will display in color on the screen lines alongside each passage of coding, named with the node that codes the passage.

There are many uses for these stripes apart from the obvious one that it is useful to see what coding you have already done.

- Print out the entire document with stripes. (TIP: use a color printer where possible to maximize the value);

- Use them in comparing coder decisions in teams;

- Discover overlapping and patterns of coding – or absence of coding – at nodes;

- Explore richness or sparseness of coding – which may itself indicate much about your data and/or your handling of it. Too much uncoded data – is your interviewing technique failing to gain the rapport sought? Did you go to sleep while coding? Very thickly coded data – is this a place where more careful probing and more time spent on a topic might have clarified themes?

- Use reports with Coding Stripes for a range of research purposes. Stick them on the refrigerator to reflect on the overlapping of themes. Print in color or drop into a multimedia presentation to impress a client. Or display in NVivo, live on the screen in a Node Browser, so you can click on the DataLinks and take the audience directly to the audio record of this significant moment, or Browse the original document to display the case that you now know matters most.

Chapter 8: Shaping data – Sets and Trees

This chapter concerns ways of organizing the data in a project, to maximize access and management.

NVivo provides many modes of management of data. But two are specifically about shaping data. Documents and nodes can be shaped in sets. And Nodes can be shaped in the node system.

These two ways of organizing data are dealt with together here because they are complementary. Node system design achieves one set of goals for bringing categories and data together in ways that assist coherence, storage and access. Use of sets achieves a quite different set of goals – grouping nodes and documents to work on them.

Neither process requires much learning. You can make a set of documents or nodes, or you can organize nodes in a node system, in seconds, using basic drag and drop techniques. This chapter is about why you might want to do so.

Overview

- Sets and node system shaping are flexible and complementary methods of management. However you shape your project in NVivo, the shape can always change as your project develops;

- Neither sets nor node system management are required by the software. Some researchers will use one or neither, and different projects will use these methods in quite different ways;

- You can make as many document sets and node sets as you like, and put as many documents and nodes in them as you like;

- When you put a node or document into a set, you are putting in an alias (shortcut) to it. And if you remove one from a set, you delete the shortcut, not the document or node;

- Sets provide convenient, adjustable, and often ephemeral ways of grouping together documents, or nodes, for some purpose — no matter how different their content may be;

- Sets are used at every stage of analysis; they can be used in coding, scoping searches and storing results. Think of sets of items as the throwaway groupings you carry around to do work with, but the document and node systems as the permanent residences of those items, where you can always go to find them;

- Documents and nodes (aliases for them) can be put into any number of sets. The Set Editors allow detailed selection and filtering of items in a set;

- Unlike the document system, the node system has structure. The node system provides convenient tools for keeping nodes in useful places so they can be found easily;

- Every node has a place in the node system and usually a node has one place;

- Nodes can be organized in the node system to make them easy to find, in specified areas of the node system or in hierarchical Trees representing categories and subcategories – much like the hierarchical index system in a library.

For instructions about handing sets of documents or nodes go to the *Reference Manual*, Chapter 8.

Shaping in sets

What is a Set?

A set is a grouping of documents or nodes for purposes of working with them together. Every project provides two sets, one of all documents and one of all nodes. You decide if you want to make other specific sets. If you create memos, the project provides a set of memos.

When you create a set, you place in it an alias (or shortcut) to each of the documents or nodes that you wish to have in that set. The item still exists in the document system or the node system – its shortcut in the set is in effect just a fast way of getting to the real item. The idea is the same as file "aliases" in the Macintosh operating system, and file "shortcuts" in Microsoft Windows. When you put a document or node into a set, it remains in the set of All Documents or All Nodes in the Explorer, and is unchanged by being made a member of the set.

There is no limit to the number of sets a document or node may be aliased to. Any item can be in several sets. This is likely if there are several contexts in which it is considered. But, one item can occur only once in any given set, and sets cannot contain a mixture of documents and nodes.

When you remove an item from a set, you are only getting rid of the alias there; the real item is still alive and well in the document or node system. And, a set can be empty.

The title of the set and its description are given by the researcher and can be changed at any time.

Why use Sets rather than other ways of grouping items?

Sets are the swiftest and most flexible and visible way in NVivo of grouping items, either temporarily or for significant stages of a project. However, they are not the only way of grouping items. For example, documents can be grouped by coding at a common node – so the node will reference all those documents. Nodes can be grouped (see below) by how you place them in the node system. Documents or nodes can be grouped by giving them common values of attributes – by looking at that value you can find all the items having it.

Sets are more useful than these other ways of grouping for many purposes:

 ◆ They are more visible – you see your sets and can manipulate them directly in the Explorers;

 ◆ They are more flexible – it is so easy to place items into and out of sets;

- Putting items into sets and removing them again doesn't disturb any organization or arrangement you have made anywhere in your project, because you are only manipulating aliases;

- NVivo provides powerful ways of selecting the set's exact grouping and evaluating it – you can filter sets and explore their features finely.

A set can be a very temporary way of juggling data items, or a structural feature of a project throughout its life – you decide how transient your sets are. They are easy to make and manage in the Explorers, and easily deleted. When you delete the set you delete of course the aliases to those documents or nodes, not the items themselves.

Uses for Sets

Sets are useful at any stage of a project. You can use document or node sets:

- To construct another set;

- To manage data, so you can see stages, progress and changes in data construction;

- To direct and inform coding. For example, have a set of the documents not yet coded, or a set of the documents coded by each of your team members, or group those nodes into a set that repeatedly occur in coding some sorts of documents;

- To bring items into a model, or save the outcome of modeling, *(see Chapter 9 Modeling);*

- To scope and specify searches *(see Chapter 10, Searching);*

- To group the results of analysis;

- To group your memos on different topics together;

- To group samples of documents of different types you wish to compare, or nodes referring to different stages or sites;

- To collect working groups of documents or nodes to manage research timetables (the work for this week).

In a team interview project, researchers might wish to compare team members' contributions. They might make a set for documents they each have authored, (including interviews they conducted and memos they wrote). A search for comments by interviewees can exclude the "All Memos" set from the scope of the search *(see Chapter 10, Searching).* To find if researchers who are trained nurses interpret interviewee comments differently, restrict the scope to the sets of documents for those team members, plus the "All Memos" set.

Most projects can use sets for keeping together:

♦ Nodes in the Free Nodes area that seem to have some grouping –
preparatory to moving them into the Tree Nodes area (see below);

♦ Nodes for themes co-occurring in data, so you can concentrate on coding
with them. You can make a "working set" of nodes and code with the set
to facilitate this;

♦ Nodes that pertain to an area of analysis (nodes relevant to the paper you
are writing);

♦ Nodes around which theoretical work is concentrating (such as privacy
themes) or for core categories being constructed.

Node sets in a project on nursing patients in pain might include a set of all
the nodes to do with pain management, a set of nodes created by the
research assistant Jane, a set of nodes to do with issues in nurse education,
and a set called "Recurring Themes". A node "Listening to Patients" might
be in all these.

Making Sets

For a technique that permeates a project, sets are easy to make and manage.
You can create sets and change their contents, (including emptying them).

♦ Directly in the Document or Node Explorers;

♦ In the Set Editors, where sets can also be manipulated, viewed and
created using filters.

Making Sets in the Explorers

The Document and Node Explorers show your sets under the Sets icon in the
left pane. Double click on the Sets icon to see the sets you have. You can
create a new empty set using the Tools menu – where you can name it and
give it a description too. Click on a Set name in the left pane and the
documents in that set will be displayed in the right pane. You can then drag
and drop documents or nodes from the left pane of the Explorer into the set,
or remove them, via the context menu.

Start a new set by dragging into it the first document you wish to place in it.
Change its title if you like, (double-click on the title and retype) and the set
is ready for any purpose you put it to!

This is a moment's task, and researchers who wish to work this way can
make and delete sets rapidly and casually. It is worth experimenting with
this technique to see if it suits you – try thinking of it as a way of putting
data in heaps, to concentrate briefly on just one aspect, or to compare
particular issues.

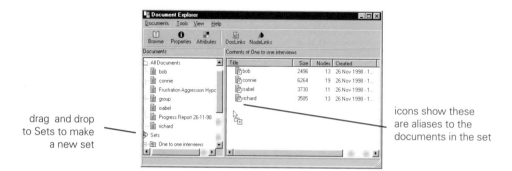

drag and drop
to Sets to make
a new set

icons show these
are aliases to the
documents in the set

Sets of nodes made that way might include working sets like "nodes that seem not to be used much in this sample" or "Free Nodes that are specific to one interview". Documents might be grouped in a set for "interviews I handled badly" or "need return visit".

Explorers provide the best way for quickly creating and populating sets from scratch. If you want to fine tune a set, or make a new set based on an existing one, you are better off to use the Node or Document Set Editors.

Making Sets in the Set Editors

In the Set Editors, sets can be made and modified by selecting particular items in one set and copying them to another; or by filtering items into and out of sets using a powerful battery of filters.

You can choose to view the set of all documents in the left pane of the set Editor, or restrict to some other set you have, such as of documents that are memos for other documents. The right pane contains those you put into the working set you are creating. One pane at a time is active, and you can copy documents from one to the other, or remove them.

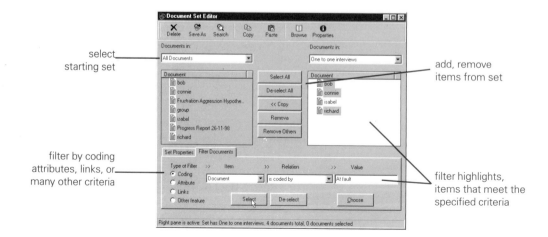

select
starting set

add, remove
items from set

filter by coding
attributes, links, or
many other criteria

filter highlights,
items that meet the
specified criteria

Filtering the set

Filtering is a process that allows you to see what is going into a set and evaluate it. In the Set Editor, when you specify a filter, the effect is to highlight all documents or nodes in the active pane that meet the filter criterion. You can do this before adding them or removing them from the set, or you can review the set by applying a filter.

> *Juggling "Select" and "Deselect" like that gives boolean combinations of filters permitting subtle probing of the properties of the set. This acts as a powerful searching tool in its own right, and in particular allows you ask and answer "Which?-" questions: "Which drivers admit fault and don't think they are good drivers?" These "Which?-" questions will be discussed more fully in Chapter 10 on Searching, where the Set Editors play an important part.*

Filtering of sets can be used to shape data very quickly for particular purposes. Want to see whether this issue arose only recently? Make a set of your memos on the issue and filter by the attribute "Creation date" to select those started this year.

To make the set you use the "Save As" button to save the documents in the pane as a set. But you may not save the set. You can use filtering simply to ask a question – did only the nurse researchers use these nodes in coding? Thus the Set Editor offers quite a new way of interrogating your data.

Filtering can also provide specific and rigorous selection of data. (Pursuing the significance of "listening" in the earlier pain management example, you might make a set of documents coded at nodes to do with a range of patient needs, then add to the set the documents with a high numeric value for the attribute "number of hospitalizations" and exclude those in the set of nurse-trained team members. Now make another set the same but including the nurse-trained researchers, and compare the two. And the filtering can, of course, be used to make the comparisons.

See the Reference Manual, Chapter 8 for detailed worked examples of set creation and filtering.

Shaping the Node System

The node system in NVivo is a different and complementary way of shaping project data from sets. In the node system you can organize nodes in two ways, by area and within two areas, hierarchically.

All node systems have some shape because they have areas. NVivo provides for Free Nodes, Tree Nodes and Case Nodes, three different areas in which nodes are organized and placed differently. As explained in Chapter 4, most commonly, Free Nodes are used to hold nodes that do not have a clear logical relationship with other nodes. When such a relationship is understood, it can be expressed by placing the node in the appropriate place in the hierarchical Tree Node or Case Node structures.

In the Node Tree, nodes are organized hierarchically in categories and subcategories. Nodes can be moved in or out of the tree, but each node has one place. (If a node is needed at two places, it can be copied, but the copy is a different node, not an alias that will update as the original is changed. Sets are normally preferred in cases like this.)

Hierarchical storage of categories

Using the ability to organize nodes hierarchically is entirely optional. It is also very natural; there is nothing new about hierarchical node systems. The majority of researchers who categorized qualitative data pre-computer (or who stored family accounts, recipe cards or Christmas mailing lists!) used Tree-structured systems, because these are helpful ways of storing and finding information. Some items "belong"under others, and coming to understand may be a process of developing, creating and placing them under the more abstract or general category. Finding them involves knowing where to look.

The majority of computer users handle their files and folders in a hierarchical node system – that's what is shown in the Windows Explorer display. Libraries store their books this way, and we find them easily, even if we have forgotten their title or author. Organized hierarchically, a node system created in qualitative research shows the shape of the emerging categories, the growing thesaurus of concepts in terms of which the data are being analyzed. In fact, in some ways a better name for the a node system in Trees would be a Thesaurus System.

Case nodes are a particular example of hierarchical storage of nodes covered in Chapter 4. These provide hierarchies that are structured differently for storing cases and case types.

The ability (not requirement!) to organize data hierarchically in NVivo is not a demand to think rigidly in hierarchical categories, top down, any more than a library catalog or thesaursus forces you to. Categories can be created in any order in the Free Nodes area, then moved "under" other categories in the Trees only if higher level (or more general) concepts are developed or discovered. Or they can grow subtrees as more specific dimensions or concepts are developed.

To use a hierarchical node system helpfully, researchers need to be clear about what it offers:

- Node trees offer a taxonomy;

- Designing trees is therefore a clarifying experience, alerting the researcher not only to where things easily "go" but also to areas that are muddy, unclear;

- A tree thus helps us not only to store things and find them again, but also to find related things easily. A well organized library is a pleasure not just because you can find the book you knew you wanted but also because alongside it are books you didn't know of but which are of related interest;

- A tree of nodes provides information about the body of knowledge it represents, and often prompts action. A library catalog will tell you in moments that this library has not been purchasing books on your specialty area, and thus suggest attention to the biases of the committee for purchasing. The recipe card box reveals your food preferences (or perhaps those of your mother). The Christmas card list shows you are losing touch with Australian friends and it is time to cross the equator. Supervisors of research projects using the NUD*IST software, which pioneered hierarchical node systems in qualitative computing, find their students' node systems offer a very helpful picture of where a project has got to, and where it needs to go now.

It is also important to be clear about what a hierarchical system is *not* offering. This is most simply summarized by pointing out that NVivo provides not only for node trees but also, since they shape data in different ways, for Free Nodes, models and sets.

- A node tree is *not* a model or diagram of connections the researcher makes between concepts on the basis of interpretation of the data. It very rarely will even indicate those connections. Using it that way will have procrustean effects on the data and is strongly discouraged.

  Example: The anthropologist studying the relation of a people to their environment discovers they have many words for water. In NVivo, the researcher might create nodes for each word, coding the different uses, and place them as children of a tree node 'words for water'. The observer of this node system would discover nothing about why there should be so many words for something described in English by one. To discover the different ways the words are used, we would have to go behind the node system, to retrieve the data coded at each node, and memos written

about each, read and reflect upon these. To explain why there are so
many different words, we need to explore these meanings in context. To
theorize about the relevance of many-worded water to the relation of
culture and environment requires much more reflection and study. To
represent that growing theory visually requires a model involving
multiple concepts. These new concepts may well also be stored at nodes
in the node system, but certainly will not be located as subcategories of
the node "words for water".

- A node tree does not do what sets do! In a useful node system, since each
  node is part of your vocabulary of concepts, each node has a place (which
  may of course be in Free Nodes, or under a Tree Node called "Where the
  hell do these go?") By contrast, a node or document (i.e. its alias) can
  occur in many sets, since sets are not a taxonomic storage system but a
  way of bundling things to think about and work on.

Designing and using your Node System

Free or Tree?

When you create a node, you locate it either in Free Nodes or in the
hierarchical trees. How to decide its location? Some guidelines:

- NVivo does not require sorting of its categories. But qualitative research
  usually does. As you draw ideas together, and synthesize, making sense
  of the data, a growing, uncoordinated collection of codes can impede
  understanding and access to categories. You'll lose them! You'll forget
  them!

- At any stage, Free Nodes can be moved into the Trees (or the Case Node
  System). What you do with them there is up to you. It might help to
  collect categories that go together in clusters. Others may be
  dimensionalized as you explore the many meanings given a concept. The
  nodes can then be reorganized, moved around, and deleted at any time.
  As patterns emerge, nodes can be collected into little trees, and divided
  into more trees as the picture gets more complex.

The case for staying Free (at least for a while)

There are advantages in delaying shaping node trees for many
approaches to theory development.

- Early specification of relationships between categories can preempt
  discovery from the data, and cloud perception;

- ◆ The Free Nodes area provides a safe holding place for early tentative ideas or apparently unconnected concepts, and helps you see them as unconnected and explore possibilities. Tree structuring of a node, like any linked diagramming, leads you to look for relationships represented in the structure.

Use Free Nodes:

- ◆ If the node has no obvious *place* in your categories;

- ◆ If you are tentative about it, wondering if this is really a *nodeworthy* idea;

- ◆ As a parking space for ideas that are yet to come together. In some research approaches, (e.g. "Grounded Theory") the convergence of categories, or recognition of dimensions of concepts is important to development of theory during the project;

Place it in a Tree

- ◆ If it has a place as a subcategory of a more general category, or as one of a group of same sort items;

- ◆ If your interest is in the range of themes in the data, or the absence of some themes, requiring their systematic comparison and differentiation;

- ◆ If the node represents one of a group that go together (e.g. dimensions of a concept, values of a variable, or types of a response) the tree expresses that relationship accurately, helps clarification of the interrelationship of concepts, themes, etc. Reorganizing, reclassifying, deleting, and combining of parts of your trees helps the developing understanding of the data;

- ◆ If swift access to nodes matters, you will find the address of a node in the Trees assists you in locating it in the tree display, developing a mental map of your categories, and in accessing them quickly for fluid and swift coding processes;

- ◆ If your node system is getting large enough to lose nodes or use them inconsistently, organizing them in the Trees will assist you to locate them since they are located by their meaning and not by their name;

- ◆ If it helps to start seeing categories in groups, making recall and access easy, meaning you find nodes easily and use them consistently;

- ◆ If you are working with cases, NVivo can help handle them if you make Case Nodes organized in trees.

When to start a Node System?

Some qualitative projects start with a considerable node system, much of which is already organized in Trees, before they have documents.

This does not imply preemptive theorizing, just that your head is not empty of ideas! Sometimes the Node System is devised "theory-down"; sometimes it merely expresses descriptive categories essential to the research design.

If you know, for instance, the questions being asked, topics or hypotheses being tested, and code at nodes for these categories from the start, you can explore emerging patterns immediately.

Checklist: advantages of working early in a node system

Nodes can be created in advance of doing any coding by very swift methods, with substantial advantages:

- Given the nodes to ask the question, you can use the Search Tool *(see Chapter 10)* to get immediate access to your data (e.g. what did the women say in answer to question 3?), to monitor progress and do data-driven sampling;

- Early recording, ordering and exploring of possible categories helps clarify the project's goals;

- Storing descriptions and memos at nodes from the commencement of the project assists research teams in sharing proposed meanings for categories and discoveries about them;

- Results of exploring and searching your node system show the state of the project, the amount of data collected in each area, and the need for new directions of data collection.

How to begin designing your Node System

If you wish to start with some nodes in your Node System, two questions to ask are:

What do you know you know? (And is it an Attribute or Node?)

Most researchers know some things about sites, people etc. (like their gender) which will require descriptive coding.

- In NVivo to record such information, you have a choice between coding at nodes, and assigning values of attributes;

◆ If you want to manage a variety of data, and especially if the data will build up fast, make an early decision about descriptive coding and how it will be done;

◆ Some researchers start a project by representing things they know about the project, or information they wish to store about respondents, in coding at nodes that will allow them to discriminate between different sources or contexts of data.

What do you know you are asking?

Most projects have some central categories they are investigating, questions they know they are asking. To express these in a starter Node System helps clarify the scope of the project, and allows you to start asking those questions sooner.

A good starting point for a node system is the rule that if you want to ask it in NVivo, you usually need the attributes or nodes in terms of which you can express the question.

Goals for a node system

◆ The node system will work best if you *see* it as a system and one that you like and can use. Try to make one that you can see the shape of in your head; explore it, draw it (perhaps in the modeler or in software like Decision Explorer) and explain it to colleagues;

◆ Node systems are usually best kept coherent and parsimonious. There's no point in having categories you forget about or only use sometimes. Use sets to manage nodes that are getting in the way. Sets called "Throw away?" and "Too Vague - shape up". Use the ability to view nodes in the Node Explorer to scan where your coding is going, which nodes are not being used;

◆ Projects are whole, and have shape. The node system is the shape of the categories in your project. As your understanding of the project develops, you may find you can draw in that shape by plotting out the major trees and branches - establishing a small set of very general and independent categories. Explore each category for related ones, its siblings and children;

◆ Projects have parts - check on your coverage and thinking about each part. Make the logical aspects of your project the basis for sketching the trees.

- ◆ Work on the categories with logic, (grounded theory methods are helpful here), shaping them into groups of the same sort of things. Which categories belong with which others, which ones are sub-cases of others, which are alternatives, do they overlap, can there be other cases of this general category? What sort of category is this? What does it belong with? Those questions help powerfully in designing node trees.

- ◆ Keep conceptually related categories together and unrelated categories apart. The most common difficulty with node systems occurs when researchers break this rule. For example, if you are developing nodes about problems in schools (authority, discipline, learning difficulties), don't allow those nodes to acquire subcategories about the settings of problems (classroom, playground, staff-room). To do so will immediately expand the size of your node system alarmingly. It will also confuse your thinking, since settings are different sorts of things from problems.

This tree combines two different sorts of items, problems and settings. It will impede category development (of new dimensions of authority, for example, and block general questions. And it is a big tree.

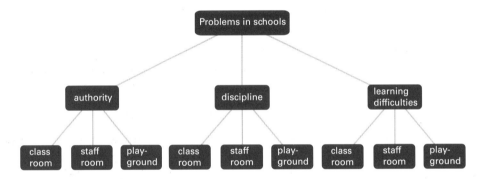

If instead you have a sub-tree for problems and a sub-tree for settings, (only 6 nodes under these!) you can code text at both the relevant problem and the relevant setting and use search procedures to find particular combinations.

These trees clarify the issues. Code as appropriate at problems and settings. You can search for relationships of problems and settings.

- Try not to make trees that build in assumptions about what you are going to find in your project. The first, big tree shown here is an obvious howler in this context – non-problem processes can happen in playgrounds, (even staff-rooms!) So these settings should not be located as subcategories of Problems;

- The golden rule is that there is no such thing as a perfect node system! A node system is always in flux as ideas change, since nodes in NVivo express the researcher's thinking about the data. An interesting discovery of many NUD*IST users is that the node system gets perfect only as they reach the end of the project. Having it "settle" is usually a sign that categories are "saturating" and a conclusion is in sight!

Qualitative researchers often wish to draw, diagram or represent visually their ideas. There may be hunches, perceived patterns or relationships between parts of their projects, discoveries in their data, ideas in the literature and tentative or fully developed theories. Ideas change and links become more tentative or more confident, diagrams build cumulatively in layers as understanding accumulates. NVivo provides a Modeler designed for such qualitative modeling.

Overview

♦ The ways of modeling in NVivo support a series of processes that researchers identify as central in qualitative research;

♦ Models can contain icons for documents, nodes and their sets and attributes, other models or new items – jointly called model items. These can have labels, comments and link lines (optionally arrowed) between items;

♦ Models can include textual commentary, including a Model Description, item descriptions and labels for links;

♦ Icons for NVivo project items in models link directly to those items with jump-to capacity;

♦ You can create and flexibly manage many such models in the Model Explorer, with display of all models, opening to show all items in the model, with ability to move between them, and view them in different ways;

♦ Drag and drop items between models or from the Document and Node Explorers;

♦ Any number of layers of a model can be selectively or cumulatively displayed, and managed in a palette on screen;

♦ Groups of items can be selectively or cumulatively displayed, and managed in a palette on screen;

♦ Styles of links and items, using color, font and border to identify them can be specified, designed and displayed;

♦ Models can be used as presentation tools for meetings or conferences, printed, saved as bitmap files, or nested as items in other models;

- If a tree or subtree of nodes is added to a model it will be displayed (if space permits) in a linked tree structure, offering an alternative view to that in the Node Explorer.

NVivo also links with another software package, Decision Explorer, which supports different and complementary modeling. You can export the nodes in your index system to Decision Explorer and map and interrogate processes. For details of how to export the nodes, see the *Reference Manual* Chapter 4. To view the potential of Decision Explorer in combination with NVivo, go to QSR's web site,.

The *Reference Manual*, Chapter 9, gives full instructions for making and changing models, their items, layers, groups and styles. It explains how to save and explore models, print them and save as bitmaps.

The challenges of qualitative modeling

In all forms of qualitative data analysis, some form of drawing is useful. Most researchers draw diagrams at analysis stage, as aids to *seeing* links, or as ways of reporting and demonstrating them. Some draw diagrams earlier than that, sketching hunches and rival theories. Visual representations of patterns and discoveries vary from tabular displays to free-form sketches, but they share the goal of aiding the researcher to see things more clearly. Some are more formal representations, for example of hypotheses, and established causal or sequential links. Sometimes these are drawn as "networks" of items linked by arrows, sometimes as spatial representation of stages, locations, or priorities.

Problems of modeling off the computer

Most qualitative researchers find modeling difficult, since the pictures we draw of what is going on in a project are loose representations of data stored and ideas recorded elsewhere. Commonly, such drawings are messy, tentative and unhelpful, often they are not used as evidence or shown in public, and researchers tear them up fast. Usually they cannot be used directly to inform analysis, since the development of a model cannot be traced through sequential stages, when links are only on paper.

Moreover, links on paper have the grave dysfunction of leading the researcher away from the data. In representing what is being seen in the project, we want both to win distance from the busyness of data and to have rapid access back to the data items that contribute to the model.

Goals of computer-aided qualitative modeling

Qualitative researchers draw and use visual representations in quite varied ways, usually requiring:

* Live models, whose links to the project items can allow the researcher to move between model and design, analysis, search, redesign and model revision;

* Layered models, with ways of representing progressive discovery, different levels of interpretation and different ways of seeing. Qualitative models are always multidimensional and researchers want to be able to move between the dimensions;

* Multi-item models that represent a range of items in a range of shapes and styles, within which those items can be grouped and displayed by group.

NVivo is designed to support drawing of a wide range of representations of data and analysis, which are linked to the project in entirely new ways. The tool for creating these representations is the Model Explorer, and the drawings are referred to as Models.

The variety, low status and unconfident use of such representations hitherto is indicated in lack of a generic term in the literature. Discussions occur under diverse titles such as "data display", "maps", "integrative diagrams". Some discussions prescribe narrower ways of drawing, (e.g. "matrices", "networks", "cognitive maps"). NVivo's Modeler supports these representations, but links them to other ways of viewing and exploring data. Models *display* data, but so too for example does a Browser. They *map* ideas, but so too does the Node Explorer. They need not be *diagrams* (they can be merely collections of related things to think about). They can be as simple as your sketch of what you think you should do next, or as complex as a representation of your analysis and conclusions.

NVivo uses the term Model to represent all of these to stress purpose not appearance; all in some way are modeling what is going on in the research.

Using the Model Explorer

The Model Explorer integrates all the functions, formatting and changing models with the display of the currently selected Model.

click on items to add items

scan, assess list of items in all models

add to model, project documents, nodes, attributes - and open them to browse, rethink

status bar gives description of selected item

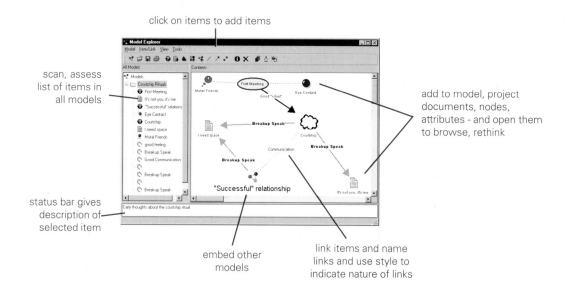

embed other models

link items and name links and use style to indicate nature of links

It lists a project's models and their contents in the left pane and displays the model in the right pane (or its contents in different views if you request to see them, as a list, or icons). Thus it can be used to review and revise what's in models, as they accrue.

Creating a model

Model creation is very immediate and simple. There are several ways of starting a new model. None of these requires that the model start with complex contents (or indeed any!). You can begin a model with one item you are puzzled about and build it up as you come to understand the item. Alternatively you can open a previous model and save it under a new name in order to adapt and develop it (or copy it and paste all or part into a new model).

New models you start will be saved until you delete them, and can be easily viewed and managed in the Model Explorer.

To create the models you need, play with the different ways of adding items to a model, representing and linking them. Links can be added, removed or altered as you wish, and will connect the items as you specify, the link being retained if you move the items around.

You can specify and change:

- Which items are in the model;

- What data they represent (without removing links to the data items nominated);

- Their appearance (color, shape, border for graphics items; style, arrow and direction and thickness for links);

- Their labels;

- Which items are linked and how;

- Which layers and groups an item is in.

From the model to the data

If a project document or node is in a model, you can jump to Browse it immediately. Having rethought it as a result of the modeling, you might wish to edit a memo or recode some data at a node. The item's context menu gives many choices. If an attribute is in a model, you can jump to explore it, view the documents or nodes with that attribute, perhaps, on reflection, change its values.

Thus icons in a model are not mere representations of your project's parts, but are directly linked to the documents and nodes in your project, and the attributes of either.

♦ Double-click on an item in a model, and you are taken to that item in the relevant Explorer or Browser;

♦ Right mouse click at the item and you can select how you view it: see its attributes, browse its text, explore its parts.

Making the model changing and multidimensional

A major design feature of the NVivo Modeler is its flexibility and multidimensionality.

Layers, Groups and Styles are provided to support researchers' needs for seeing parts and processes as well as the whole. These tools do different things and can be combined as needed to:

♦ Break models into simpler views and bring them together;

♦ Zoom in and out, from detail to the "big picture";

♦ Construct a cumulative picture of change;

♦ Contrast different interpretations of data;

♦ Dissect or build up explanations for viewing and discussing or displaying;

♦ Simply create visual effect!

You can review and select which layer or group or style will be displayed at a time, and can always return from the partial picture to the whole.

Styles of model items

NVivo allows researchers to nominate, describe and specify the appearance of *styles* of items or links in a model.

> *Styles are a feature of the cognitive mapping tool, Decision Explorer, that links with NUD*IST4 and NVivo. NVivo will export nodes directly to Decision Explorer. You can use the NVivo Modeler for some representations of the project, and export the nodes to Decision Explorer and define the same styles in both programs.*

Appearances do matter, if display is your purpose! Experimenting with functions of the Modeler may assist you in making the appearance not only striking and thought-provoking but also to reflect change and development.

- Design icons (from the item's Properties Box), specifying color and style, or perhaps a bitmap image of person or setting the item represents, or as a clipart cartoon;

- Turn an icon into a text box: set its shape as a rectangle with its label inside, and give it a long, label;

- Use color to group functionally related links in your model; use the same icon shape for thematically similar items (a cloud for vague thoughts – whether the item is a node or a document);

- Make important items with heavy borders, show strong relations with thick lines. A dotted link is very tentative!

Layering of models

A model can have any number of layers, and you can manage them rapidly for exploration or display. Any layer can be viewed alone or with other or all layers.

Layering is very important to record visually the development of a project or different perceptions and interpretations. Model layers support management of variety and change in a project. Different types and purposes of models will get layered in quite different ways. Here are a few modeling ideas with quite different layering:

- You can use different layers to show different relationships between the same objects. In a model of office workers where their case nodes are model items, on one layer put the communication channels between them, on another the flow of work, on a third the authority links;

- You can put items on several layers. Have a layer for the union members, another for the employees, another for the managers, another for the process workers. Joe might be on three of those layers;

- Display sequential stages or samples and their features or results. You can start a first layer of a model before you start a project, and most researchers will use many such models at the planning stage, or later to account for the process of project development. Copy the latest layer to make a new one for the next stage of the project, add new document and node items to it, link them in, change earlier links as new results indicate, and then go back to the earlier layers to see how your interpretation has changed;

- Show different team members' impressions of the same material in different layers, and compare and bring them together for discussion. Combine the layering of a Team Picture Model with filtering sets of nodes from different team members;

- Build up a composite picture of how several "local" theories together explain the situation;

- View and reflect on the different interpretations by different actors in the field.

A Layer Palette allows you to select to Show Layers as you wish – one, all or a selection. In the team meeting flick between different ways of seeing the problem. In a presentation of your project work, show sharply the different results of policies. You can jump to all the data behind any item, to scroll and discuss.

Grouping model items

Groups in many ways are like layers – you can take items in your model and put them in one or more groups, and/or layers. But whereas showing a layer or two gives you a selective view that excludes everything else, when you ask to see a particular group on the currently visible layer(s) you see the members highlighted in boxes. You can nominate any model items to be placed in named groups, and can define the group.

Groups and layers are independent of each other. Importantly, you can have groups cross-cutting layers. For example, in an historical study, the layers of a model might represent time periods, and the groups social classes. In the NVivo "Doing Rustic" Tutorial Project a model might show different ways of seeing Annie's life history: layers for years represented in her diaries, groups for the central issues in her life (links with the Old Country; demands of nineteenth century marriage; isolation and deprivation of early bush life.)

- You could use a Model to design the project, later adding documents, nodes, attributes as you create these, nominating Groups for each stage of the project (or perhaps for each set of documents if you are using sets this way). Later, if you want to create nodes or attributes as indicated by the model, view the model items as lists to assist rapid setting up of the project;

- You could use Groups to highlight the factors most important to different influential people in a situation being studied;

- Different groups of items might belong to different subprojects in a multi-site study;

- A palette allows you to select to Show Groups as you wish. (Combine with the Show Layers display tool!).

> *A well-styled multilayered model with different groups of items defined for each section of analysis and layers for each stage of a project, makes a great computer-based medium for a meeting or conference presentation. Show your project with a projection pad.*
>
> *Use colors and styles to make the visual impact impressive. Have a "core" model for displaying your project work. Select bitmap images of significant people or sites to represent the items. Run the presentation in NVivo, and you can at a mouse-click call up the Browser on a Node to answer a question about the evidence for your conclusions, or on your Project Document to account for the research process and jump from DataBites to the videos of the opening group interview...*

See the *Reference Manual*, Chapter 9, for a worked example of a model using layers and groups. In a study of a workplace, layers show format, informal and hidden relationships, groups show different employment areas. Displaying different layers and groups shows crosscutting pictures of process and relationships.

Storing, exploring and revising models

Saving models is of course available (indeed the Model is saved until you delete it). But most researchers are not helped by accrual of multiple long-forgotten models. If you wish to save models, the options to name the model and write a description should assist you in differentiating them.

The option to Save Copy As allows you to start a model with one already designed, altering it appropriately. Try using this option to sketch how a situation would be interpreted by several different theories.

Returning to models during the project is immediate – in the Model Explorer simply select the required model (and if appropriate the required layer(s) or group(s) of items).

Invent methods to make a model contain images of change. For example:

- You can nest an earlier model as an item within the present model, so your account of how a theory developed can contain (and jump to) the early image of its development;

- Save sequential versions of a model as part of an audit trail accounting for development and grounding of your theory. Save as bitmaps and use them as DataBites in your audit document.

Where does modeling fit in the research process?

Most qualitative researchers create diagrams at several different stages of the research process - hence do different things. But without software support, most of those diagrams remain unlinked to the project.

NVivo is designed for researchers to create and store webs of models, develop them, move from model to data, to questioning processes and pattern seeking and back to models. Many analysis paths can be followed, and these will usually be combined, for instance:

* Modeling leads to project design and development, e.g. construction of new nodes to represent discovered concepts;

* Coding of a document leads to a model exploring its case or context, and creating of sets of nodes;

* Modeling leads to analysis processes using the Search Tool, pursuing suggested links;

* Analysis outcomes produce data that can then form the basis of a model; for example a display of time ordering of events with date attributes, with corresponding data displayed in a Matrix Node set, which can be shown in live tables;

* Comparison of models over time, or of different cases, leads to further search process, and a new synthesis model and combination of previous models leads to memoing and synthesis via an integration model.

As with all qualitative methods, the use of models will differ with the methodological approach. If you have not used models previously, because the tools were not available to you, you may be helped to exploit them by reading texts that describe their use more fully than this book can do.

Most researchers have developed modeling skills that assume models are either static, once-off episodes or change only at the cost of mess. Consider using models for new more fluid processes. Sketches of the ideas being brought into a project or discovered in literature can start a project. Research design models help teams coordinate - and later to understand any changes from the original proposal. Analysis models need not be at the end of interpretation.

The following tables suggest possible uses for this qualitative Modeler at different stages in a project. It is provided particularly for researchers who have not hitherto found modeling supported by their data analysis procedures. It is of course suggestive only. As the tables show, almost all these uses of the Modeler will lead to a fluid series of changing models, and comparative analyses of them.

Preparatory Stages

When might you use the Modeler?	Research Proposal model	Literature review Model
Why would you use it?	Reviewing prior knowledge: getting down your ideas so they don't bias the research.	Discussing previous research, gaps, rival theoretical approaches and methods.
What things are represented?	Actors or processes being researched, early ideas about links between them.	Research sites, projects, stages, fashions, theories. Layers identify items in common and differences.
Where are you coming from?	Sources are early project proposals, hunches, reading.	Literature and discussions, project proposal preparation.
Where are you going to in your NVivo project?	Sketching early index system.	Early sketching of research designs, piloting, and early coding.
Future use of the model	Evaluate growing understanding, development of Index System and its categories.	Put assumptions in context, conference about project, team planning etc.

Research Design Models

When might you use the Modeler?	Research Design	Tree diagrams	Teamwork model
Why would you use it?	Visualizing the process of the project, proposed project stages, samples, funding.	Setting out frame of coding categories.	Clarify and discuss team roles.
What things are represented in this model?	Stages, questions being asked, goals, problems anticipated, sample attributes.	Nodes - linking groups of items into a catalog of categories.	Layers for team members, their expertises and contacts.
Where are you coming from?	Project proposal or grant application stage, pilot study.	Clarification of nodes and documents.	Early formation of teams.
Where are you going to in your NVivo project?	Project Document with DocLinks and NodeLinks to plans, spreadsheets etc.	Setting up a starter Node System.	Developing skills and ability to coordinate in using the software.
Future use of the model and what tools are needed?	Review progress, add layers, alter and store e.g. monthly reports.	Starting Tree structure.	Review and report.

Analysis Process Models

When might you use the Modeler?	CONCEPT CLARIFICATION	COGNITIVE MAP	CAUSAL NETWORK
Why would you use it?	Exploring relationships of categories and processes.	How one perceives the processes, events etc.	Showing possible cause-effect relations.
What things are represented in this model?	Ideas, concepts, project categories.	Representing participants' perceptions.	Processes, situations etc. and their perceived causes.
Where are you coming from?	Messy data: this is a clarifying task.	Trying to see things as the other sees.	Expressing hypotheses or emerging explanations.
Where are you going to in your NVivo project?	Revising categories, writing memos, new layers.	Involvement, understanding, interpretative work.	Weighing and enriching explanations.
Future use of the model and what tools are needed?	Build up, comparing cognitive maps of participants.	Compare, develop such models.	Towards a more qualitative explanation?

Analysis Presentation Models

When might you use the Modeler?	CATEGORY DEVELOPMENT, ANALYSIS PROGRESS.	TIME SEQUENCE MODEL	INTERACTIVE DIAGRAM OR REPORT.
Why would you use it?	Dimensionalizing, distinguishing features, where you've got to, what's needed.	To see events, processes in time sequence.	Understanding and concepts in the big picture
What things are represented in this model?	Histories of categories. Layers for earlier versions of theory.	Events, stages (of a life, a dispute, a war.)	Concepts and memos, model comments.
Where are you coming from?	Developing index system, recoding hypothses.	Show sequence clearly; link events, model reshapes data.	Display
Where are you going to in your NVivo project?	Clarifying, restructuring project.	Framing the story, using date attributes.	Refinement of a sequence of models. Final report.
Future use of the model and what tools are needed?	Theorizing; archive versions of the model.	Stick it on the wall!	Account of theory development.

10

NVivo takes a new approach to the multiple ways researchers wish to search data and ideas. It is designed to assist the researcher in asking natural questions, as well as powerfully framing the analysis. Search processes, ways of focusing searches and choices for using results, are integrated in one tool. The Search Tool allows specification of search operation or outcome in terms of the processes of data management and exploration described so far in this book.

Qualitative researchers rarely ask only one question, blind, broad sweeping questions, or single-dimensional questions. So they are not helped by a data handling method that reduces them to questions like "give me all the text coded at the category for Pain Management". They usually want to ask more exploratory questions, like "When trained nurses talk about pain management, is there a sense of control that has to do not so much with training as with years of experience and particular areas of expertise? Which care areas am I sensing this in and how do those nurses express it?" The Search Tool in NVivo is a device for helping you frame and check that sort of question -then ask it of your data.

Overview

◆ The Search Tool provides a wide range of flexible options for searching qualitative data. This one tool integrates all the familiar ways of searching data, plus some new ones, so that researchers can apply any of the available techniques in the one search. To specify a search using the Search Tool, you:

1. Choose the operation "*What do I want to ask?*",

2. Set a Scope "*Where do I want to ask it?*" and

3. Specify the context and formats of results "*What do I want to do with the results?*".

4. ... and then, still in the Search Tool, you can check the results, modify the recipe for the search, and do it again -exploring or building on the results of the first search.

◆ Text search is fully integrated with searches of coding and attributes;

◆ The ability to scope a search provides for accurate focusing of the question or just the data you want to ask about. The scope can be changed to ask a slightly different question. A scope can be specified items of documents, nodes, or attributes, filtered as you wish;

* The scope tool can be used, without doing a search, to code or investigate any documents, nodes or sets;

* You can do coding by searching. Results of searches of nodes, text or attributes can be coded at any node you specify, with the context you specify;

* You can Assay any items in a scope. An Assay provides a profile of the items according to documents, nodes, attributes or text you specify. Assay allows you to ask "wh-?" questions, "What have I got here?"

* Search results can be customized, and can be saved as nodes or node sets which in turn can be assayed;

* You can create a **matrix** in the search tool. The resulting matrix table can be viewed "live" on the screen, with cells shaded to give visual representation of data patterns. Click on a cell to view the text it refers to. You are taken to browse the node that codes the data belonging there.

Full instructions for using the search tool are in the *Reference Manual*, Chapter 10. This contains details about each process integrated in the tool, the operators for text and coding search, the ways of scoping searches, the process by which you can assay a scope and the options for saving and using search results. Read these instructions to ensure you get full use of this highly integrated tool.

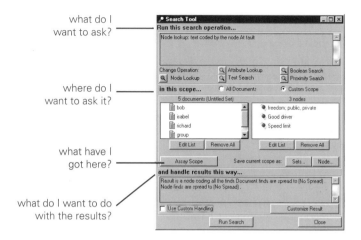

what do I
want to ask?

where do I
want to ask it?

what have I
got here?

what do I want to do
with the results?

Understanding Searching

The search tool is designed around the sort of questions you ask yourself
when exploring, reflecting on, probing patterns in, and puzzling about
qualitative data. These questions are rarely simple.

NVivo's Search tool is designed to *integrate* a wide range of ways of asking
these more interesting qualitative questions (as well as the simple ones) very
directly. Previous software (including NUD*IST4) separated out technically
different search types, such as text searches on the one hand, or looking for
coding on the other. NVivo combines these types together so you can express
without technical restriction the sort of inquiry you have in mind. The three-
part setup process for a search directly supports the intellectually natural
way of posing any inquiry: "look for *this here* and *present* my finds this way".

This natural structuring of search queries, without division between search
technicalities, encourages you to *say* your search requirements, as you think
through the data puzzles you are pursuing. Think up a question, say it in the
Search Tool, and you are probably using at least half of the processes
described in this book. You can tell the Search Tool, for example, to:

Find text coded by the node "drug abuse" or containing the text "drug",
"heroin", or "cocaine". Look only in documents with the values "suspect"
or "previous record" for the attribute "Sample group". Finds should be
spread to the surrounding section. Keep the finds from each document
separately, in a series of nodes, one per document. When done, assay
the results quickly to see what features they have. Now redo the search
changing the attribute values to "witness" and educator" sample groups.

What do I want to ask?

You nominate a search operation to define what to search for. In specifying it, you can call on combinations of coding by a node and text search (as the example in the Overview section above shows), and also the values of attributes. These three types of search are available individually. They can be used jointly in the so-called relational searches, Boolean and Proximity. They are available for joint use since a question you ask may naturally involve any or all of the three search types. The example above would use a Boolean search, Union.

You first choose which of these five groups of operators you want. Together they represent many different ways of searching. When you have chosen your operator, choose the nodes, attribute values or text search patterns you want it to operate on.

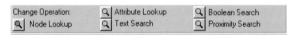

The simplest search operators are the first three. They look up just one node or just one attribute value or search for matches to one text pattern.

Two remaining search options offer groups of Relational operators (Boolean and Proximity). These offer different ways of asking questions about the *relations* between coding at nodes, the values of attributes and text patterns. You choose the operator you want, then select the nodes, attribute values or text patterns you want your chosen operator to apply to.

Where do I want to ask it?

Qualitative researchers usually wish to specify and shift the context of a question or reflection. This is done in NVivo by choosing and changing the scope being considered. Even the simplest of searches -looking for the coding of a single node -can be focused by specifying which documents and parts of documents (coded at nodes) are to be searched. With this simple search, scoping can reveal the "fine structure" of the node being looked up. Or the scope tool can be used without doing any search, to code or assay any documents or nodes.

You need never set a scope for a search; the default is all documents, no nodes (i.e. all of all documents), but you will usually want to. Scoping allows you to point a search, or do comparisons, and then to rerun the same search, and study the different outcomes.

To select the documents and nodes for the scope, the Search Tool takes you to the multi-purpose Set Editors for document and node sets. Select and filter the documents and/or nodes you wish to search. Once you've built the scope you want, you can code it at a node. Coding might be your sole purpose, or you may wish to save this scope for future use in a different search.

... And what have I got here?

But how do you know you have a scope suitable for your search? Maybe, by the time you've built it using all those filters to get rid of irrelevancies, there's nothing there! So you might want to find out first what sort of data is in that scope, before applying your search to it. The Set Editors can deal with a lot of those questions, but another and rather different tool is Assay.

The Assay tool reports on the scope items in terms of coding or attributes. This means it has very wide uses. It is a different kind of analysis to Search. It can be used to discover patterns, see through confusion or to explore shapes in data. It can be used as a filter on scope items – change the scope, assay it, tweak it again, assay it.

What do I want to do with the results?

You do not need to customize results at all. Let the search run and collect the finds into a node and show you the text. If you wish to see the results in a particular way, or save them for another purpose, explore the options to customize:

- ◆ You can tell NVivo to display your finds one by one as they are discovered on the spot, for your consideration;

- ◆ You can ask to have the results of the search spread to a useful context;

- ◆ You can specify which nodes the results are coded at;

- ◆ You can have results for each item searched saved separately so you can immediately read and compare them;

- ◆ You can rerun Assay on your results, to see where your results occur in the scope items. This is a new and very powerful way of assessing results.

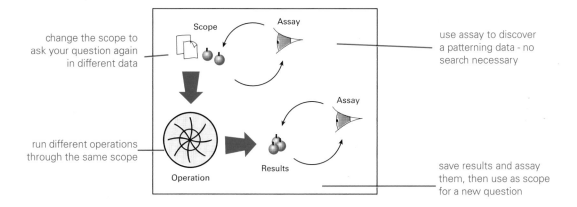

change the scope to ask your question again in different data

use assay to discover a patterning data - no search necessary

run different operations through the same scope

save results and assay them, then use as scope for a new question

To summarize, a search with NVivo can be simple or as tailored as you wish. The search tool is designed for quick questions; say what you want to ask, leave scope and results at the defaults and Run Search. But NVivo's Search tool is also designed for ongoing discovery and the building up of cumulative understanding. Searching in qualitative research is an iterative process of asking questions and trying to find the answers, discovering and trying to find and test the patterns that "make sense" of your data, and building on earlier hunches and discoveries to construct bigger understandings. Thus it requires that hallmark of social science research - system closure, the ability to save the answer to a question as more data, so another question can be asked of it. Results are data, and the ability to save the results appropriately can be very helpful.

Search in progress…

The walk-in approach to integrated searching described above allows exploration of data in a quite different way. The process of setting up a search operation can be of value whether or not the search is carried out. Using the Set Editor and its filtering procedures to set up a scope can in itself give analytic insight -*see Chapter 8*. Then, once the scope is set up, it can be explored using Assay, to understand it better and check its suitability for the intended search operation. You might find before you actually do a search that the scope contains no documents – and this is your answer! Or you might explore by changing the scope. Studying how isolation in rural areas affects education, I might move through searching, scoping and assaying in this way:

Question to ask	Search Operation (What am I asking?)	Scope (What do I want to ask it of?)	Result Format (What do I want to do with the results?)
1. How does isolation affect education?	Single node lookup to get all text coded at **schooling problems**.	Case Nodes with Attribute value **Location = isolated**	Make a node, browse, read and think.
2. Are women's experiences of this different?	Same operation.	Restrict the previous scope to interview documents with attribute value **Gender = female**, run the search. Then rerun with **Gender = male**.	… some differences in what they say - but mainly the men seem to say less… (Spread nodes to include context.)
3. Is this because the men really have no direct experience of home schooling processes?	Same operation.	Time to Assay each scope. Profiling by the node for teaching roles, I find…	Men do have a part in it, but clearly a different experience.
4. Is home teaching at the centre of the stories of isolated schooling as a positive experience?	Boolean Intersect to get all text coded at **positive schooling experiences** and also at **home teaching**.	Flick scope again between the men's and the women's interviews.	Women's stories about home teaching are not mainly about tasks, more about sharing knowledge.

Using the Search Tool

Whether or not you have used qualitative computing software, this is a new way of expressing and doing searches in a naturalistic way, "close to the question". To get into it quickly, explore each panel separately. Start by framing questions you want answered. Think through the logic of different operators and apply them to nodes, text searches and attributes. Leave the second and third panels (Scope and Results) untouched; by default your search will apply to all documents and be saved as a node.

Framing a question this way, qualitative researchers usually find they want to direct it to some particular data. Explore the Scope panel separately, experiment with making different scopes and coding them. Change the scope of documents or nodes by editing the list. Assay the scope to find out about them. Scope can be used for groping around, feeling your way in unfamiliar data, coding it or reshaping it – as well as scoping searches.

Now scope a search, and run it without customizing results. Critique what you get. (The Violence Prevention tutorial takes you through such processes in stage 2.) It is likely that the mechanical process of searching has not retrieved the context or saved the coding that your interpretive processes now require. This takes you to the option to customize the search results. Try out the different results of spreading and evaluate the retrieval.

If you have been using NUD*IST4, you will find all of its Text Search and Index System Search operations (and some new ones) available within the one Search Tool in NVivo, one way or another. NVivo adds attribute-based search, replacing reliance of "base-data coding". Their integration means that they occur more easily in combination, as may well be required by the questions you are asking.

NVivo incorporates the N4 abilities to **restrict a search** to documents or text coded at a node, via the idea of scoping – but allows very many different sorts of restrictions and importantly the combination of restrictions, to specified documents, coding or attributes.

Assay is new. To ask which data was represented in N4, you had to make a node and conduct other search operations on it.

Using various operators, Vector and Matrix searches occur throughout the Search Tool, as particular ways of searching using ordinary operators. Results can now be saved as individual nodes for each cell, and viewed in a new live matrix display on the screen – click on the cell and browse the text coded there.

Now for the details! The following sections describe the search operators, the scoping functions together with assaying, and the ways of saving results. *Full instructions for the processes of specifying searches are in the Reference Manual.*

Search operations

To start a search, choose one of these five options:

- ◆ For Boolean and Relational searches you then choose from the particular operators of that type;

- ◆ Specify the items the search will look for (the operands);

- ◆ Choose the format for storing the finds.

The Simple Searches: Node or Attribute "Look-Up" and Text Search

These are simple in the sense that they have only one operand – a node, attribute or text pattern. The first two don't sound like searches – they simply take you to one node or one attribute value. You could of course go to these in the Node Browser or Attribute Explorer. The fact that they are here in the Search Tool reinforces how much more it will do than just carrying out a simple retrieval. You may want to ask questions about the occurrence of just that node or just that attribute value in various scopes. You may want (using result formatting) to find which scope items have it, or divide the finds on the basis of which scope items it occurs in. Such questions can take the form: "I'm trying to understand in what contexts this innovation is rejected", or "If the speaker is an inner-city resident, what sort of attitudes will I find?"

> Why no Single Document Lookup to get the coding of scope nodes into a given document? This is the same as a Union search on those nodes, with that document as scope.

Looking for text with one node's coding

Node Lookup finds the coding by the node you specified, in the scope documents and in the text coded by the scope nodes.

Note: you can get a related but different result by assaying that node in the scope; like Node Lookup, this will find all scope items with coding at that node. But Node Lookup gives access to the coded text.

Looking for text with certain values of an attribute

Attribute Lookup requires you choose an attribute of documents or nodes, then specify the values you want to find.

If you specify the value of a node attribute, it looks through the scope items for passages coded by any nodes with that value. If you specify a value for a document attribute, it will find the scope documents with that value.

This allows you to select finely. NVivo allows number or date attribute ranges to be specified. If you're interested in what the under-25s have to say in your conversational transcripts, you have scope nodes coding the speeches by people in the transcripts, and those nodes have a numeric "Age" attribute, then you can break out the under-25s with one Attribute Lookup - just set it at "Age < 25". And if you wish "Age<25", "Date>October".

Text Search

Text search can be simple or very subtle. The integration of text searches with all other searches means you can naturally ask questions about coding, attributes and what is in the text together. Text search is also very accurate, because it finds exactly the characters where a text pattern occurs and it can be pointed to exactly the scope documents and passages coded by the scope nodes you want it to search. For passages coded by scope nodes, the find is strictly of matches that that lie fully inside passages coded by the scope node.

NVivo's text search tool is based upon the well-known concept of so-called regular expression text parsing, or grep, but with extensions for NVivo's documents. As you would hope, if you tell it to look for "Russian Constitution" it will look for all passages in the scope with that text phrase, or string as it is usually called.

- ◆ Text searches may specify *where* accepted finds will be made. For example, specify finds at the beginning of paragraphs or sections – useful if you start a paragraph, or head a section, with a speaker or topic name. Or specify that finds should include Links, or be at the beginning or end of words - useful for finding stems and other grammatical fragments, or complex discourse;

- ◆ Text searches may specify if they are case sensitive or not -so the above pattern could match the string "Russian constitution", or things from a crazed typist like "rUSSIAN cONSTITUTION";

- ◆ Text searches can be restricted to whole words or phrases, so that the above pattern won't match in the text string "Byelo-Russian Constitutional Convention". Useful if you are seeking "sex" and want to avoid London's home counties;

- You can specify alternative matches, such as "cat" or "dog" if you are interested in pets. At the character level, this provides features of interest to linguists;

- You can throw various wildcards into the patterns, which will match a range of things. One use is to find one expression followed, at a distance, by another one -there's a wildcard that will match the padding in between: the ".*" in the pattern "cat.*dog";

- You can specify a level of approximation in your matching, at up to 9 mismatches but still catch the quarry. The pattern "Mackey" (non case sensitive) will match "Mackay" at an approximation level of one mismatch, "Mackie" at two, or "McKay" at three. Useful for dealing with bad spellers, but set the mismatch count too high and you'll catch garbage.

Details of wildcards and patterns are in the Reference Manual, Chapter 10.

Using text search

Text search can thus be used as a "quick and dirty" way of finding a quotation, locating and coding every instance of an expression, a name, or an issue. Select Text Search, type what you seek, leave the scope at all documents, and run the search. The choices for saving results (see below) allow you to use this technique to "auto-code" finds – or simply to locate the quotes, browse them and print them off with context, delete the node.

Alternatively, text search can be a very sensitive way of exploring the nuances of meaning in your data. Use scoping to point the text search into different parts of the data, for example to ask about the words different members of a company use in describing the process of change you are studying. Search for any of a group of words restricting the scope to the managers, then change the scope and search for the same words in the interviews with junior staff.

Text search can also be an efficient data manager. For example, if you are commenting on the discourse used, set the scope to all documents that are memos and search for a particular observation in your notes, in a particular context. Annotating transcripts in an interview project, you might have a convention that you insert, where appropriate, a phrase like [*contradiction*]. A simple text search can find all and only such occurrences and you can specify (see below) that with their sections they be coded at a node for contradictions observed.

Text search combined with specification of scope documents and nodes may be used as a finely tuned research instrument, seeking and finding all the occurrences of words, phrases, hesitations or any other aspect of a document expressed in text. Where do contradictions occur? By specifying a scope (say, all documents that are group discussions) and then changing it to run the same text search in a different context (say, all individual interviews, then all interviews in which the respondent has expressed confusion) you can ask questions about the contexts of contradictions and how they operate in different settings.

> The text search facility in NUD*IST4 can be combined with index searches in a series of moves to achieve some of the effects of scoping the search, but each move requires a new search. The ability to assay the scope, asking who's saying this, is new and powerfully extends the uses of text search.
>
> If you have been using N4, you will find that the integration of Scope with text search makes it much more inviting as a way of exploring, a serendipity tool. Change the scope, assay it, change again, assay, and you will swiftly find where these words are occurring.
>
> Coming from N4 or any other qualitative software, you will also find a major new set of analytical tools in the ability to include text search and attribute values in relational searches.

The Relational Searches

There are two groups of searches using combinations of two or more single node lookups or single-pattern text searches, or attribute values.

◆ Boolean searches: – the "and", "or", "not" and "less" searches;

◆ Proximity searches - which find items that are near, preceding and surrounding other items.

NVivo provides a logically full range of these searches and, as mentioned before, they can be carried out using any of the three types of search jointly; looking for passages coded by a node, looking for documents or nodes (effectively, passages) with a particular attribute value, and looking for text strings matching a text pattern.

NVivo also supports making a matrix using appropriate relational operators. All of these operators are detailed below.

Why use relational searches? Most users of qualitative software are familiar with at least some of these searches; those that ask questions about combinations of coding. NVivo now allows you to ask about the relations between one node, text string or attribute value, and another. Most questions you want to ask about qualitative data are about the relations of categories - otherwise you are effectively doing code-and-retrieve on isolated unrelated categories. At best, you are relating them in your head after you retrieve them. In NVivo, even if you just use the lookup search types, you are still actually doing a type of relational search-intersection, because of the scoping facility.

Boolean Searches

There are four operators in this group: "and", "or", "not" and "less". NVivo also lets you make a matrix using two of them, the "and" and "less" searches. As with the Search Tool as a whole, you "talk" the search you want. Select the right operator, then nominate which items – nodes, attribute values or text searches – you want to apply it to.

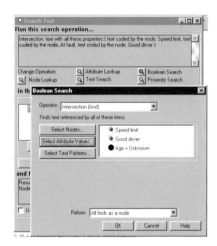

The dialog requires you to nominate the items you want to carry out this search on -nodes, attribute values and/or text patterns. Some of these searches ask you for *two* groups of items, not just one as in the Intersection dialog shown above.

Operator	Upper group	Lower group
Intersection (And)	Find text referenced by all of these items	[not relevant]
Union (Or)	Find text referenced by any of these items	[not relevant]
Negation (Not)	Find text referenced by none of these items	[not relevant]
Difference (Less)	Find text referenced by any of these items	but not by any of these items
Matrix Intersection	Find text referenced by each of these items	pairwise with each of these items
Matrix Difference	Find text referenced by each of these items	pairwise less text referenced by each of these items

Choosing and using the Boolean searches

Intersection is a way of narrowing down your picture, since it finds the text referenced by *all* input items. Intersection is picky, it gets only the data that everything you specify applies to. It's easy to end up with no finds at all if you use intersection. Remember, coding or text finds may be only a few characters.

In fact, intersection is often too narrow a search. It will miss adjacent passages from the input items, and the intersections it finds are often only sentences or even parts of sentences. For this reason, it is a good idea to spread finds from intersections to the surrounding paragraph, or even section. To avoid missing adjacent items use an appropriate Proximity operator instead, e.g. overlap. You can see the differences in any Coding Stripes display in a Browser.

Explore the input items available. For example, intersecting text search and node coding finds where certain words are used in the context of a particular topic. Intersect text search for "Mackey" at an approximation level of 3, with the node 'Drug deals' in a scope of witness interviews, to see if someone with a name like that was mentioned as involved in drug dealing. You'd want to spread the finds a good deal though!

Union is a way of broadening your picture, finding the text coded by *any* input item. Use this to unite several topics for joint scrutiny. A common example is to unite a bunch of sibling tree nodes; for example the seven children nodes of "Deadly Sins". Then you can look at them all together. Similarly, you may want to form the union of all the nodes in a set, or all documents in a set.

The ability to do this means you can code at specific nodes. If you've coded a wicked act as "Gluttony" you don't need to code it with "Deadly Sin" as well -you can get at the deadly sins in their entirety at any time by uniting the individual ones.

Union is also useful for housekeeping. Nodes that essentially mean the same thing, like "Schizophrenia" and "Split Personality Syndrome", can be combined without losing coding.

Negation is the flipside of Union. It finds the text coded by *none* of the input items. This is usually an enormously broad operation. The union of a few items plus their negation is the entire scope! Usually, negativity is better handled by the next operator, Difference.

Difference helps distinguish between one category or group of categories and another. It finds all text in the union of the first group of input items, but not in the union of the second, subtracted, group of input items. This makes it a useful way of finding finer-grained concepts amongst the coarser ones. For example, if you want to study the onset of maladies in your patients, and you've only coded for maladies and treatments, start with all the nodes coding the various sickness reports ("Cold", "Eczema" and so on); then subtract the nodes describing treatments, cures and outcomes ("Giving Pills", "Recovery", "Death" and so on). What's left? Descriptions of bouts of sickness without the description of treatment and outcome -the onsets you were interested in.

Note: care is advised in spreading the results of a difference search like the one just described, or you might let back in a lot of the material you subtracted.

Difference has a rather different effect when it operates on attribute values. Since these apply to whole documents, or whole nodes, Difference will find scope documents with any document attribute values in the first group, then remove the documents with attribute values in the second group. And correspondingly for scope nodes. So this has a filtering effect rather than a slicing effect.

Using Intersection, then Difference on the same pair of items (item A intersect item B, then item A less item B), provides a good way of dividing item A in two. This is sometimes called "sectioning A on B". You could use this sectioning to find where someone with a name like "Mackey" is talked about in connection with drug deals, and where they're talked about out of that context.

Intersection and Union function identically to N4's searches of the same name, except that they can include attribute values and text searches as items in NVivo. Union supports the particular search called Collect in N4 – the union of coding at a node and all its children. Negation is the same as the Not-In search in N4, and Difference as the Less search. Scope and Assay add further analysis opportunities.

Matrix Versions of Boolean Searches

Matrix is also very new in NVivo, both for what you can ask and for what you can do with it. Matrix is available for two of the Boolean searches – Intersection and Difference. Suppose you have nodes in your project for various speakers you have recorded, and those nodes code their speeches. You have given those nodes demographic attribute values; for example the node "Mary" might have "AgeGroup= 30". You have coded the transcripts with the topics people discuss in them, such as "/Topics/religion", "/ Topics/politics", "/Topics/sex" and "/Topics/sport".

If you wanted to be thorough in your comparative analysis, you would compare one age group's text on a topic, with the other age group's on the same topic. Matrix intersect takes on this boring repetitive task and does it in one hit.

The items to intersect can be individually chosen. As in NUD*IST4, you could select the children of "/Topics" and the children of "/Attitudes". In NVivo you can select any nodes and just some values of one attribute, and a text search. Matrix will then carry out the pairwise intersections on the *m* number of objects in the first group and the *n* number of objects in the second, and store the resulting *mn* number of intersections as sibling matrix nodes - a special sort of tree node that knows its place in the matrix and how it was constructed.

In this way, Matrix Intersect will give you a rigorous distribution of material according to coding on any collection of nodes, attribute values and/or text patterns cross-tabulated against any other collection. Thus you could ask for reasons for leaving by age group, or attitudes to authority. You can then browse the resulting matrix nodes to study the contents of each one, or look at them in a table. The live matrix display is described later in the chapter.

Proximity Searches

These searches are often the preferred ones for qualitative researchers, whose interest is less in the logical relations of categories than in their more fuzzy relations. In the dialog, you tell NVivo two items to operate on – nodes, attribute values or text patterns. With Matrix versions, this becomes two groups.

Operator	Upper panel	Lower panel
Co-occurrence (Near)	Find places where text referenced by this item	is near text referenced by this item
Sequence (Preceding)	Find places where text referenced by this item	starts before text referenced by this item
Inclusion (Surrounding)	Find places where text referenced by this item	surrounds text referenced by this item
Matrix Co-occurrence	Find places where text referenced by each of these items	is pairwise near text referenced by each of these items
Matrix Sequence	Find places where text referenced by each of these items	pairwise precedes text referenced by each of these items
Matrix Inclusion	Find places where text referenced by each of these items	pairwise surrounds text referenced by each of these items

Choosing and using the Proximity searches

Co-occurrence looks for where text from its two input items (for example passages coded by two nodes) occur in the scope items, and in particular looks to see if a passage from one occurs near enough to a passage from the other. If it does, that's a find.

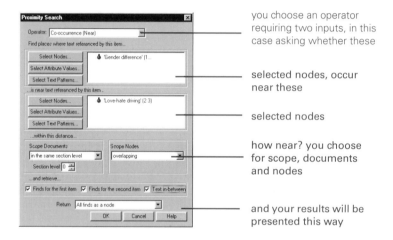

you choose an operator requiring two inputs, in this case asking whether these

selected nodes, occur near these

selected nodes

how near? you choose for scope, documents and nodes

and your results will be presented this way

How near is near enough?

You choose. For a scope document the choices are obvious enough -you can require finds from each item to overlap, be in the same paragraph, or be in the same section of a level you choose (0 means the entire document). Scope nodes contain, in general, several passages from several documents. For them you can require the two items two finds to overlap, be in the same paragraph, or be in the same coded passage.

What do you want to keep?

The goal might be to use one of the inputs to Co-occurrence just as a locator for the other. For example, a market researcher might be interested in talk about the product's quality in any section (discussion segment) where there's talk about competing products. Only those passages are requested, not the talk about the competition. Of course, if they overlap, bits about the competition will be included anyway. Sometimes both passages are wanted, and any connecting text between them.

A primary use of Co-occurrence is to find where two topics are associated in some thematic way, e.g. by a train of thought or association of ideas, in the text. Co-occurrence is thus a relaxed and flexible version of Intersection. Intersection will find only passages from two inputs that are so near they overlap, and then it will only hand back the overlapping part. Two topics are rarely discussed *that* closely together. The Overlap version of Co-occurrence finds the intersections too, but hands back the *union* of the passages that intersect, not just the bit where they actually intersect. This makes overlap a particularly useful form of co-occurrence, as it will retrieve the whole conversation within which two themes occur, or the whole text passage where two cases are discussed together.

Wider versions of Co-occurrence, for example in the same paragraph, will net more finds, but of course the train of thought between the one topic and the next in the text will get more tenuous, and may even break. Checking each find as it is made can be useful here.

It is worth considering the different results these different nearness specifications give. Compare "Give me everything said about the managing director if they are coded as talking *in that passage* about leaving" with "Give me everything said about the managing director if anywhere in the same document they said they were leaving". The latter is more likely to retrieve text where the managing director was irrelevant to the job switch, but the former will not get everything the leavers think about the managing director.

In a study of traditional family ideology, the researcher might use Co-occurrence to explore the assumptions about home ownership and family life. Where people are answering separate questions about these topics, and where their interconnectedness is not discussed, the themes rarely intersect, yet they co-occur consistently.

Sequence is just like Co-occurrence, except passages from the first input item must begin before passages from the second. This will find, not just associations of ideas in the text, but where one idea leads to another.

> Co-occurrence and Sequence integrate the searches in N4 called Overlap, Near and Followed-by. Proximity can be more finely specified in NVivo, and Scope and Assay add further analysis opportunities.

Inclusion finds a different sort of relationship, in which a passage from the first input item encloses a passage from the second. Technically, it will find all pairs of references from A and B, provided that the A reference starts at or before where the B reference starts, and the A reference finishes at or after the finish of the B reference. Perhaps you wanted every mention of the managing director that occurs in the context of a discussion of why they are leaving... For scope documents, this occurs in the same document, and for scope nodes it must be in same retrieval passage.

Inclusion integrates the searches in N4 called If-inside and If-outside, with Scope and Assay adding further analysis opportunities.

Inclusion gives slightly different options for the retrieval range, compared to the previous two proximity searches. Ask for the passage from the first (surrounding) item and get the entire find (what were the reasons for leaving, that they should talk about the MD?). Or retrieve just the passage from the second (inside) input item (what did they say about the MD in this context?).

Proximity searches are in general far more useful and flexible than Boolean ones. Most researchers could do most searches required with Proximity; but if restricted to Boolean searches would be quite handicapped.

The Matrix variants of the Proximity searches allow running many proximity searches together, exactly as Matrix Intersection does. Matrix Proximity searches are however likely to be of greater value for qualitative inquiry. They will hand back whole comparative tables of idea associations, trains of thought, or contextual relations, on the two series of input items.

Scoping the Search

You have chosen the question you want to ask, now where do you want to ask it? You can do this in fine detail by setting a scope for the search.

Setting the Scope

Qualitative researchers usually wish to point searches at particular bodies of data. NVivo innovates by allowing fine detailed specification of the scope for a search.

The scope for a search is simply a set of documents, and/or a set of nodes, whose text will be searched. If the required set exists, it can be selected as scope. Sets are created using the Sets Editor, and so the Search Tool simply calls it when you ask to edit the list of documents or nodes.

Most of the time, you won't have exactly the right sets for your scope. This is because you've just thought up a question for framing a search, such as "I'd be very interested to know if people who've had immediate contact with cases of drug abuse feel the same way about safe-house programs as the general public." You need to isolate the transcripts of people with that experience. The Search Tool takes you to the Document or Node Set Editors to select particular documents or nodes, or sets of them. Using the filter you can highlight and view items according to their attributes, their coding or other criteria (such as owner, date, even icon color). Then, if you wish, add or remove them from the set you are building up to be the scope for this search. When you have the scope you want, click Search and you are taken back to the Search Tool with that scope in place.

Sets, and the fine-grain way you can make them up, are described in Chapter 8. See also instructions in the Reference Manual.

Perhaps I am studying the different acceptances of curriculum innovation in a range of schools. I might be tracking down the very different responses of teachers in different authority situations. I want the coding at "rejection of new curriculum" and "feelings of powerlessness" if these co-occur (near) in the same section. But I want this first for the teachers in the lower status school where I started the project.

I want to ask my question about the documents in the first of my multiple field research sites. They are a set that I made a while back. I add to the pool nodes coding where people in other sites discussed the teachers from schools in the first site. The pool now includes everything from the first site and also everything about the teachers from that site. However this scope would be too broad. I don't want interview documents that came from talking to students or parents. So I filter to remove documents that have the attribute value: "role=student" or "role=parent".

Saving and Reusing Scopes

What to do with the scope you have crafted so carefully? You may just run the search and throw it away. But note it is persistent, the next time the Search Tool comes up it will have that scope. So this focus for your questioning can be maintained. Pursue the attitudes those first-site teachers have to innovation in general. Is their conservatism due to lack of resources? What do they say about wish-lists for funding? The same scope can be re-used or adjusted, in subsequent searches.

There are options to keep that scope. The two sets (documents and nodes) can be saved. Name carefully so you can reconstruct your line of inquiry. Alternatively, save the scope as a node coding all of the documents *and* nodes in the scope. You now have a new node that codes everything about teachers in first site. It might be prudent to include in the description field for that node, how and why it got constructed.

By including filtering by attributes, coding and other features, NVivo permits fine detailing of searches. In designing your index system and attribute system, it is worth considering the power of scoping searches. To return to the Schools Innovation project, I could not broaden the pool of my scope beyond the documents from the first site if I had not created case nodes to tap all the talk about these teachers.

Assaying the Scope

What's in a scope? You are about to search the scope, and it can be useful to get clear just what sort of information you have in the scope, before proceeding. "Which age groups are represented by these conservative teachers in my scope?" "What other attitudes do the scope teachers show to curriculum?" The Search Tool provides an Assay Tool for checking features of your scope, before proceeding with the search.

The simplest way to see how Assay works is to open it on the scope of a search. What do you want to ask about? Select items from the left pane and add to the right pane. Select one to see (bottom left corner) how many of the scope documents and nodes it is present in.

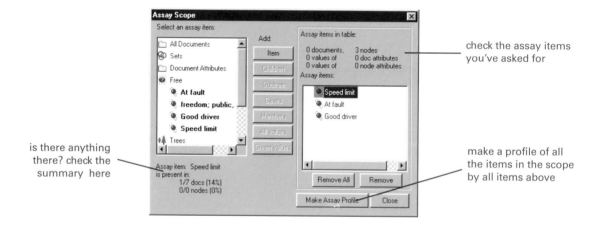

is there anything there? check the summary here

check the assay items you've asked for

make a profile of all the items in the scope by all items above

Wh-Questions

Assay supports the answering of so-called "wh-" questions. These stud qualitative analysis. *Which* schools have this problem, *which* people are saying this, *what* contexts are these comments from? Most software searches are not like this – the researcher has to say what they are looking for (Does this school have this problem? does that one, does the next one?).

How does Assay answer wh-questions? When you have accumulated several "probe" Assay Items in the right pane, press "Make Assay Profile". This makes a "presence-absence table" of the assay items as columns against the scope items as rows. The "1"s in the table show the presence of the assay item in the scope item. You can now see *which* scope items the assay items are present in. A few statistics summarize the table. You can export the table in tab-separated format for use in statistical packages, spreadsheets and the like.

these items are in your scope

these nodes were selected as assay items

cells with "1" indicate coding for that document at that node

Now if in our mythical curriculum research project we had a scope of teacher interview documents, and set up as assay items the "AgeGroup" document attribute values; then the table would show us which teachers were in which age groups. (The wh-question was "Which age groups are represented by these conservative teachers in my scope?") Add in as further assay items your nodes about various attitudes to curriculum, and you can now answer the other wh-question "What other attitudes do the scope teachers show to curriculum?"

Of course, in that table you can not only see *which* age groups and attitudes occur (their columns have "1"s in them), but you can see *how frequently* they occur. You might even suspect interesting patterns relating age groups and attitudes. Time to send the table off to a statistics package.

> *Start with one puzzling issue, sense of need for change (I have a node for this, but am unclear about the data coded there). Assay the scope on this one: on the screen I get a table of all documents and nodes in my scope showing whether or not they are coded by that node. Add further nodes to be assayed – the whole set of nodes for attitudes to change – and the table is now revealing, a clear pattern of some attitudes' dominance showing.*

Handling Results

The options for handling results vary with the search specified. There are two aspects to this:

- ◆ The results format – which depends somewhat on the search operator you choose. In the Search Tool you decide on this when you set up the search operation. The common format is to collect all the finds into one node, but other options open up interesting methodological opportunities;

- ◆ The presentation of the results. Do you want to check each find as it's made? Do you want to save the result nodes in a special place or with a special name? These are set in the bottom panel of the Search Tool. References can be spread to different levels of context, nodes can be returned as a set, or just as nodes, and stored where you choose, in the tree-node system as siblings, under a new or existing node.

As you explore, often the process of category construction and theory "emergence" in qualitative research requires small forays into the data, reading what is found, seeing it differently, rethinking the question, readjusting the lens focus. Results format and presentation options can be useful here.

> *Think in terms of what you want to do with the results of the search – rather than seeing the search as an end in itself. Are there other questions to be asked? Is there a memo to be written? No need to keep it as a node unless you wish to use it further. The output in the Browser can always be printed, and the node deleted. Or copy and paste the text in the Browser into a new NVivo document and make that a Memo.*

Spreading: what context do you want to include?

The ability to spread your finds to the surrounding paragraph, section or whole document or coding allows viewing or coding them in meaningful context. "Narrow" searches like text search and boolean intersection, can yield fragments of sentences as finds. They mightn't be very illuminating, plucked out of context; so save them in a suitable context.

The ability to spread results makes search, especially text search, a flexible autocoding tool. This can be used for very rapid data preparation and access to imported data from the start of a project; for example, for automatic coding of the answers to particular questions occurring in different places in the data; exploring data, pursuing hunches, gathering material about a topic for browsing and recoding.

It can be interesting in itself to know what the results of such text searches are, but it can be much more valuable to save those finds at a node spread to give context. If you want to find out what people are saying about their boss, you can create a node for such text, for example "/TalkAboutPeople/boss". Then a pattern search for "[boss|MD|Managing Director|manager]", spread to paragraph, could have its finds stored in that node. And when you browse the data documents you can add, to that node, references to people's boss that escaped the text search.

> *Suppose your scope is interviewee nodes (coding everything a person has said, everywhere), you could carry out a search and spread the finds to the entire interview document containing a find. So now, you get back a node coding all of those documents - you've brought them together for further study. You can then easily make a set of those documents.*

How do you want the results?

When you carry out a search in NVivo, the results are normally collected into one or more nodes and kept in the Tree Node system, instead of merely displayed – as with any normal database system. Why?

1. They are kept for later reference;

2. They are genuine data, so should be in the project database in their own right;

3. Most importantly, by being kept at a node, the coding is available as a component of later searches, and so becomes an ingredient in further questions you can ask. For example, the node can be the basis for including or excluding documents from a later scope (e.g. if you want to search for something only in interviews in which people mention their boss). Or it might be a component node in another search;

4. Since text search results can be saved in a node this means that some document coding can be done by the very fast process of text search. To speed things up even more this can be done for whole batches of documents and whole sets of keywords, without user interaction.

Making the choice

Finds from a given search operation can be collected and returned in one of these three ways. You decide:

- Single Node Format -Union all the finds together in a *specified node*, for example, a node that codes all the Site 1 ideas from teachers about innovation. This may be a new or existing node. Retitle it and keep a memo accounting for its construction;

> *Advantages: you can look at all the finds together in the Node Browser. In a subsequent search you can take all the finds from the original search and analyze them together in some way. This is the familiar form of system closure pioneered in NUD*IST.*

- Node for each scope item -To preserve the individuality of the items in the search scope, save the finds from each scope item in *separate nodes*. Their description fields record their origin automatically. These nodes will be stored in the tree node system as a siblings under a parent which holds the full search details. For example, I can obtain nodes recording what each teacher from Site 1 thinks about innovation – individually, one node per teacher;

> *Advantages: the origins are kept separate, making it easier to explore and compare the results individually. Those results nodes from the individual teachers would make a great input to an assay, or a matrix search, exploring the different characteristics of those attitudes.*

- Set of Scope items with finds. For example, collect together all the teacher interviews (scope nodes) where my search was successful – all the teachers who had this characteristic approach to innovation.

> *Advantage: often you're not so much interested in the exact text found by a search, as in which items you're dealing with (scope items) are like that. Note the wh-question logic coming in here. Find all the teachers who have this approach, and make a special study of them.*

These are importantly different results formats. The first hands back what is of interest *in a lump*. The second hands back what is of interest *in each scope item*. The third hands back whole *all of the scope items* of interest.

Assaying the results

Another very useful aspect of results presentation, is to immediately assay your results. If you ask for this when setting up the search, then on completion of the search, the Assay Tool opens on the original scope and the output node or nodes as assay items. So an assay table will show you *which* scope items your results occur in. Wh-questions again.

A note on System Closure

This ability to store research results as more data is known as system closure. It is central to much qualitative research, which can be seen to be an expanding system of information that includes ("closes in", the mathematicians would say) results and findings with the original field data - to remain as material for the ongoing research process. (Arguably, "hard" science lacks this feature). NUD*IST pioneered the support of system closure in qualitative software design in its earliest release in the mid-1980s, by storing the results of searches as nodes. With these techniques now well established, it is hard to see how software can deal with qualitative analysis in any reasonably rich way without supporting system closure.

NVivo has greatly extended this support, by providing these three ways of storing the results of a search. Moreover, NVivo's treatment of memos as exactly the same as any other document, adds greatly to system closure. A memo is not just a commentary document linked to a "primary" document – it is just as primary as the original. You can code it, and you can link it. No difference.

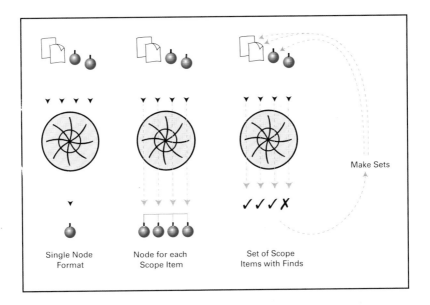

Single Node Format — Node for each Scope Item — Set of Scope Items with Finds — Make Sets

Using the live matrix display

Matrix Search produces a quite different results format from the above – a special matrix node for every cell in the matrix. This means that NVivo offers the ability to go straight to all the text coded at any cell, and explore, recode and recontextualize that text with all the facilities of the Node Browser. The nodes for each cell are stored under a Matrix Parent Node in the tree node system that records all about the construction of the matrix. The individual nodes record their individual construction. But you can access them directly from the table on the screen.

Run the search, or select a Matrix Parent Node to bring up a special tabular display, called the Matrix Inspector, of the nodes in a matrix.

choose what
you see in
each cell

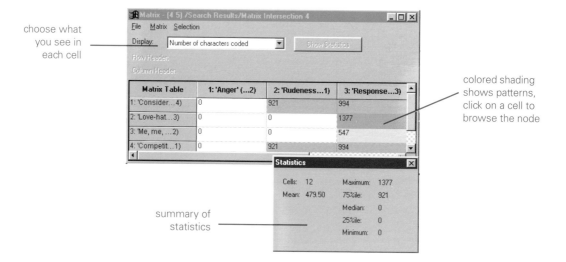

colored shading
shows patterns,
click on a cell to
browse the node

summary of
statistics

Each cell represents the node created in the Matrix operation from the input nodes referred to in its row and column headers. Now you can go, live, to the text coded at any cell, or explore the pattern of cells. For qualitative researchers, the ability to go live to the text in a cell is often crucial. In the Matrix Inspector double-click on a cell and bring up a Node Browser on what is coded there. Explore, review, re-code, widen context as you wish - this is a normal node, and all the facilities of the Node Browser are available.

To explore the pattern of cells, you can adjust the display to show the amount of coding in that cell in different ways – the number of characters, passages or documents coded. Color shading of the cells gives you a visual impression of the relative amounts in each cell – the more the darker, with white meaning none. A statistics box provides a summary of the quantities across all the cells. The display can be printed, and each of the numerical displays exported as tables in tab-separated format to explore in packages such as Microsoft Excel or SPSS.

These various coding displays and their color patterns provide a third way of answering wh-questions alongside assaying and using the "set of scope items with finds" results format for searches. Here what we're looking at is "Which of the first bunch of input items to the matrix search are related to which of the second bunch, via the search operation I used?" And the answer is more subtle that the boolean yes-no of NVivo's other two ways of handling wh-questions. In this case we can look at "Which, and if so how much?"

> *Example: in a scope of documents from interviews, we run a matrix search on attitudes to a range of issues versus a range of personality characteristic attribute-values. An appropriate operator would be Inclusion – looking for attitudes expressed in speeches from people with the different personality characteristics (note the people are not figuring as individuals in this search). The resulting matrix certainly shows us not only which attitudes get expressed by people with which personality types, but also a numerical indication of the extent of those expressions in each case. That, for certain well-distributed interview structures, may provide valuable pointers to further exploration of relationships between personality types and attitudes in the area being studied. Certainly, we have here a remarkable way in which purely qualitative analyses can provide data for the statisticians they probably couldn't get in any other way.*

Making Searches for your Purposes

If you are new to this sort of searching, it is worth reflecting on the different purposes to which searches constructed in the Search Tool might be put and how they fit together as a suite of well-integrated tools to craft the product you want.

Gathering data

Some of these searches are ways of gathering material up to rethink and reevaluate (and maybe recode) it. Co-occurrence with an overlap or same-paragraph nearness restriction is a highly useful search at the exploratory stage since it finds topics occurring tightly together, so you can make sense of why these topics did so.

Union gets everything coded at any of the nodes you specify (that's the same as copying them all and merging coding at a node). You get a lot of material, but perhaps this is useful when you are still trying to see shapes in the data.

> One Union option is to *collect* up all the coding at any tree node below the node you specify, its children or even its subtree. Let's have all the text coded at any of the different reasons for leaving. Now ask bigger questions with this new node by changing the scope (Do women and men sound different when talking about leaving – whatever their reason?).
>
> Union also strongly supports recoding, as projects mature and broader categories emerge. Example - Collect up all the text coded at specific reasons for leaving and then browse the new node, coding on into new reason-for-leaving categories like "career reasons" and "personal life reasons". This can make it easy to replace outmoded divisions by better ones. Collect is a separate search operator in N4, but the more flexible ways of selecting nodes for Union mean no separate operator is required in NVivo.

Dissecting data: an extended example

Teasing themes apart is a different qualitative goal. Several operators dissect your data, giving you access to just some material, and rigorously establish patterns of coding in your data.

To locate just where you are hearing this theme, or to test a hypothesis, you would need ways of finding *only* data whose coding exactly fitted your specifications. Intersection and Difference, or more powerfully and flexibly, the Proximity operators, will test a hypothesis that can be properly expressed in terms of coding at nodes, attribute values or text patterns.

How can this be done? Here's an example of finding and testing an hypothesis and framing of searches.

1. State your question. "Could dislike of the managing director be a women's problem?" The implication here is that gender matters.

2. Check if your project has data items for handling such a question. Nodes exist for dislike and where the MD is a topic. *Women*: a value "female" for the node attribute "Gender". *Problem*: remember to read the text to find if it is a problem.

3. Re-express the question in the NVivo project: "Are passages expressing dislike of the MD uttered only by women?"

4. In the Search Tool:

   • Operation -Use Intersection, or better Co-occurrence with Overlap, on the nodes "/Attitude/dislike" and "/Topic/MD".

   • Scope - nodes with attribute value "Gender=female".

   • Results format -for the moment lump all the finds together in one node.

5. Run the search. Yes, it brings back lots of material, so we can say women's interviews contain these topics without going any further. Is it widespread amongst the women? Assay the result node against the original scope. A good half of the women are hostile to the MD.

6. But is it only *women*? The real test of an hypothesis is the counter-examples - reset the scope to "Gender=male".

7. Rerun the search. This time we get far less material back, and an Assay shows there are only a couple of the male employees involved. Now to work with the text and the more subtle issue of whether the dislike of the MD is a *problem*. If so, why is it a women's problem, and *what* is their problem with the MD? Do the men who dislike him say similar things? Search the Results node to read what they say. To compare it with what is said by women who don't dislike him, rerun the search at step 5, and make a set of the scope nodes that had finds. Use the Set Editor on the scope as a set to remove all the nodes in it that are in the scope-nodes-with-finds set, and you have the nodes for the women who *don't* dislike the MD. Put them in the scope to see what they say. And so it goes on, refining, comparing, and making great use of previous results *via* system closure.

Limits of Search

With the Search Tool you can ask any question you can express in terms of coding at nodes, values of attributes or text patterns. You can focus the inquiry by any of the means available, to filter a set of nodes and a set of documents down to exactly the scope you want.

The limits on such searching are thus the limits of your system of nodes, your system of attributes and their values, and your access to the text. The search operations are only as good as these aspects of your project.

The search operations are also, significantly, only as good as your coding. As with any sophisticated tools, the GIGO principle applies (garbage in - garbage out!) It is important to remember that in all the examples given above, we were asking questions about patterns of coding, and attribute values, and strings of characters in documents. These have a relationship, only possibly a strong one, to patterns of attitudes to the managing director, people's reasons for leaving and so on. But NVivo cannot find the time she mentioned the managing director if she said "that unspeakable fool", and you did not code the phrase with the node for the managing director. The program cannot locate an overlap of that with her confession she is leaving not in protest but for a holiday if she never told you that, or if you missed the significance of her talk about the holiday and did not code it at the node for "reasons for leaving".

These warnings are only another way of pointing to the essential issue of the researcher's agency in qualitative research.

Coding reliability checks are often very helpful to support interpretation of Index Search explorations. (See Chapter 3 section on Duplicate Documents).

If your codes are inconsistently used, or inadequately developed, or if your coding is scrappy, be careful to make the limitations clear when you interpret results of these very fine-tuned search tools.

If coding is done by someone other than the researcher doing the analysis, use the memos and definitions of nodes to ensure that you remain in communication about the changing meaning of a category.

11

The chapters of this book describe first the parts of a project – documents, nodes and attributes – then the processes – linking, coding, shaping in sets and trees, modeling and searching.

Once you are familiar with these ingredients, your project will take shapes that are determined, not by the structure and functions of a software package, but by your methodological approach and research goals. Your next project will be different again, because it probably has different goals. And the parts and processes of any project will be constantly changing and cumulatively developing. So no project will ever look like an outline of this book, just as no gourmet meal looks like the list of ingredients and directions in a cookbook. To stretch the analogy further, most researchers, like most gourmet chefs, use recipes only as challenges not rule books. And most get beyond the cookbook rapidly.

Overview

This chapter has two goals. It offers a brief account of the crucial choices, discussing for each the ways of doing things. It also presents a selected summary of the ways of doing central tasks and the ways they are integrated. Use it to inform choices and to scan the other techniques you might consider at any strategic point.

- There are three principal ways of discovering and developing categories in NVivo. Make **nodes**, and explore what's coded at a node, make **Memos** and use the **Modeler**;

- There are three principal ways of **recording the links** you see between data and ideas – **coding**, using **DataLinks** and **modeling**;

- There are three principal ways of coding: **Visual coding, attributes** for descriptive coding, **coding at nodes**;

- But coding is not the only way of connecting data. There are three principal ways of **bringing together data items** in NVivo, and these are also ways of parting or differentiating data; **coding at nodes**, giving values to **attributes**, and placing nodes or documents into **Sets**;

- Ordering and organizing is done by **Sets, Trees** and sometimes, in different ways, by **Modeling**;

- Each of these choices provides several ways of working that are integrated with the core analytical processes of creating and filtering **sets**, scoping and conducting **searches**, and **modeling**;

- ◆ Viewing and pattern finding can be done in many different ways with different options in Browsers, Explorers, Profiles and the special Matrix tool;

- ◆ Linking with statistical data is done by importing and exporting matrices and exporting profiles and reports;

- ◆ The software is designed to support the building of a project as data are created, and ongoing analysis as data are explored. By creating and editing compound documents, the researchers can hold a project together from the start and account for the analysis at the end.

Choices and choosing

NVivo's tools and the processes they support are individually described in the preceding chapters. But as each chapter makes clear, the tools and processes are interconnected. Research design for NVivo is a matter of deciding the combinations that suit your project. The software offers choice for most processes, and making that choice requires seeing the options.

This concluding chapter looks at the toolkit differently, from the point of view of the researcher approaching the tasks of a project and choosing the best tools for particular purposes. It offers checklists of ways of thinking your way into a project or, once in, approaching a challenge or framing a question.

In creating and conducting a project, you will be constantly making choices, since NVivo is designed to offer choice. These choices can be trivial or of major importance. There are usually several ways of doing what you are trying to do. How you choose is a matter not only of methodological approach and research goals, but also of research style, researcher priorities and research timetables. And the choices are not independent – how you choose to handle your categories emerging from your data, for example, will affect the options for scoping searches. Each choice contributes to the history of a project, and to your own cumulative research experience. So how you put together the tools and techniques the software supports will be very personal. Like gourmet cooking. But the analogy again is useful: great chefs experiment, innovate, but always take seriously the range of options and the ways they fit together.

NVivo is best learned by using it and users will discover ways that suit their methods by trial and occasional error. But being informed of the choices available, for particular choice-points in the project's trajectory, will inform your trials and help avoid error.

Discovering and developing categories

In qualitative research the central task is usually the development of categories, concepts and ideas from the data. These then have to be handled in such a way that they can be stored, not lost, managed, explored and developed into theories, grounded and tested in the data.

There are many ways of creating and recording ideas in NVivo:

◆ Make nodes! Nodes in NVivo are the containers for topics, concepts or any other category for thinking about the data. Use Free Nodes to gather things that don't fit with other things. Use Trees to gather things that do, creating new subcategories for finer dimensions. Coding-on from the node allows (even forces!) you to make more nodes. Use the Node Browser to explore data coded at broad categories, rethink it as you review it in the context of the other material about this concept or topic;

- ◆ As nodes are created, or as you browse and edit documents, make Memos about them, and make those memos live, compound documents that link to other data, other ideas. Use DataLinks to link the memos to the data items they are about;

- ◆ Use the Modeler to sketch possible new concepts, brainstorm them in layered models and make nodes of those that make sense for your purposes.

Linking data and ideas or categories

There are three very different ways of recording the links you see between data and ideas – coding, using DataLinks and modeling. Each of these works for different purposes:

- ◆ Code it! Some concept-to-data links require gathering of all the material about a topic so you can review it and reflect on it, or explore the relation with other topics. Use visual coding for rapid identification of topic, source etc. or to introduce another 'layer' of interpretation that crosscuts coding at nodes;

- ◆ DataLink it! Some linkings require more direct pointers (jump from this passage to that related one, or – this topic goes with that one). Use a DataBite whenever you might wish to go to another file, or other media for displays of the idea. Use a DocLink whenever another project document expands on this or adds understanding. To link with a particular extract, make a NodeLink with an Extract Node;

- ◆ Model it! Use a visual model rather than recording coding or hyperlinks if you want to see and play with the links between data and ideas. Use models as sketch pads. Use layers, groups and styles to make models multidimensional, and to crosscut your complex picture so you can focus, discriminate and see through the complexity.

Choosing how (and whether) you code

Most researchers are familiar with coding as the principal, even only, way of linking data to topics, concepts, categories. For most it can be an onerous task. NVivo is designed to support many modes of flexible coding and remove the reliance on coding at nodes.

Usually, the response to the qualitative need to bring together material about a topic is, Code it! Usually this means we should place references to it at a category. In NVivo, such coding is more intuitive, swifter and more informed by visual displays of coding already done than it has been in previous software. Coding also combines with linking and visual coding, since both rich text editing and DataLinks are live in the Node Browser when you view the coded text. Code DataBites in documents (especially Proxy documents) to ensure that all material will be retrieved. The Node Browser permits fine selection of context and supports coding of exactly the context required. It provides the same range of coding techniques as the Document Browser to support coding-on

So why code any other way? Coding at nodes fulfils the researcher's needs to gather and view material according to interpretation, and re-view and recode it. But other methods do different things with coding:

- Code at nodes for any tasks that require retrieval of all the text coded there, or any tasks that require rethinking and coding-on of retrieved material or search of coding. Code when you want to be presented with complexity – all the different ways this theme occurs! – and when you need to resolve complexity – by coding-on to finer categories;

- Visual coding is the old method of marking-up text, discarded as researchers moved to computers and now again available because of the rich text capability of NVivo. Use visual coding for exploring material and identifying it by content, speaker etc. as well as for annotating and shaping it so it looks different.

  Use visual coding for early exploration, textual analysis, clarifying the sources or types of textual data, and above all, for editing in your ideas before they get lost;

- Assign attribute values for information you want stored, when you don't want the text returned, but you want NVivo to "know" the gender, age, school district etc. so you can review the sample, enquire about the age groups of students by school district. Most researchers have had to use coding to record such information, and to gather items together to think about them. Attributes and sets are new tools for such purposes, designed to bring data together in ways that do not fit easily with coding.

> Use values of attributes to store what you know about documents or the person, site, historical event or other data item represented by a node. Use attributes for any information that is single-valued ("base data" information). Use the absence of a value at that information as data! You can ask questions like "Which historical events have no exact date?" or "What do I know about the attitudes to politics of people whose voting intentions were never given?"

To code or not to code?

But should you be asking not just how to code but also whether to do so, or at least whether to do so now, for this purpose?

Hitherto, qualitative computer programs have emphasized one form of coding, by recording references to text at categories (nodes). Computer programs have made it a dominant, even in some areas hegemonic, method. This method is not widely discussed, and not at all criticized, in the qualitative literature. Most texts that talk of coding give it far less emphasis than most users of computer programs do. Concern at the overuse of computer-supported coding has been expressed (including by the team at QSR) in recent years. Themes in discussion lists have included how to know when to stop coding, concern at the time spent on coding, the tunnel-vision and linear research designs that result from seeing coding as a stage that has to be got through before interpretation can occur. The troubles that especially novice researchers get into with coding are easily understood. Coding is the easiest thing to do if you can't think of anything else to do to get started. Coding has immediate results, and that makes it seductive. You make categories, accrue references to text at them, can immediately be searching for patterns of coding. Novice researchers assisted by computer programs with no limit on node coding can code for ever. Qualitative methods, on the other hand, rarely require this sort of bulk coding.

If this is a methodological debate you are concerned with, you will find on the QSR website a list of regularly updated references.

NVivo supports node coding in all established ways and many new ones, and it offers the new option of combining node and visual coding and integrating them with other ways of recording and exploring links between data and ideas. But above all it offers alternatives to coding for the tasks we have strained at when coding was our only tool - bringing data together and teasing it apart.

Bringing data together

There are three principal ways of *bringing together data items* in NVivo; and of parting or differentiating data for comparison or pattern seeking. Each can be used either for short term framing of questions or quizzing your hunches, or in the long term as part of the task of managing data and gaining an overview. Not surprisingly, two are coding at nodes and giving values to attributes. The third is placing nodes or documents into sets.

♦ Use nodes not just to gather text on a topic but to point to occurrences of themes, for any tasks that require location of where a topic is raised, or of everything about a case. Remember, nodes can have attributes, so if a theme, institution or person recurs in your data, coding that material at a case node representing it/them allows you to store information about the person, institution etc;

- ◆ Values of attributes can be used as pointers to all of the documents with particular characteristics, or to all the material coded by a node representing something with these characteristics. Think in terms of gathering up and pointing to material; remember the Set Editors allow you to ask for ranges of values, thus gathering them in one place e.g. items with age greater than a particular number or dates before a particular time;

- ◆ Make sets for documents or nodes that go together (for project management purposes, for staging inquiry, for identifying team contributions, for putting aside the ones you will not handle in this paper…) A document or node can go in as many sets as you wish. Use sets for fleeting questions, as well as major shapes.

These bringing-together tools can of course be combined. Coding brings up one crosscut, attributes another, sets another. Just add color if this is not enough choice! There are system sets in place (document memos, for example, are a set). Using icon color, in the Set Editor, I can easily search all my black memos.

You might use node sets to keep aliases of nodes about a particular type of case, or use attributes to distinguish them. This has an advantage for some projects where case types are not exclusive. Consider the situation where resident activist Sue (from Chapter 4) leads a double life, working in the Urban Planning Department whose plans are opposed by the residents. NVivo does not mind if a case node for Sue is under the Case Type Node for resident and *another* Sue case node is under the Case Type Node for bureaucrats. But these are different nodes, and the system will allow them to develop differently, with different coding, links and so on. If you want everything about Sue coded at both, you will need either to code twice or to copy one node to the other. Alternatively, keep one case node for each person, and use sets or attributes to identify their residency, work status and so on.

Differentiating Data

The bringing-together tools are also the tools for differentiation of data. You can use any of these to specify and scope searches, specifying retrievals and excluding or focusing on only some data. You can use any of them to profile and assay items.

There is usually a best choice. To take a simple example, in a mixed method project you need to be able to ask for all your material on a topic in field notes, as opposed to literature reviews, interviews and correspondence. Your technique involves mixed source documents – after the interview transcript you record field notes, for instance. You could have a document attribute "Data Types" with value "Field Notes", but this would differentiate only whole documents that are all fieldnotes. This is a job for a node! At the node for "field notes" (probably under a node for "Data Types") code any full documents *or parts of documents* that are field notes. (N4 users are familiar with this technique as the software provides a node for "Annotations" so you can use searches to get all your annotations on a particular topic.) You can of course also code there any inserted text in a document that you want to have field note status, for example observations in an interview.

The challenge of choice usually has a best answer. To take an example, to use node attributes for storing information about a multi-valued characteristic (for example, if an individual plays two or more roles in a school) requires multiple attributes, since each node can have only one value at an attribute. This task would be better done coding (a node for roles can have subcategories for each role and the text can be coded as many times as necessary). But the act of coding takes more time than placing a node in a set, and aliases of the individual's document/s or nodes can be in as many sets as required. Each would do the task, but in a different way; use nodes if you want to retrieve and review the text, Sets if you want just to know which roles this person is in.

Ordering and organizing

Most tools in NVivo have data management purposes, but three are particularly designed for ordering. Sets and trees are different and complementary. Models offer another sort of management.

◆ Use sets to order data visually (a set for each stage of the project, team member or for all the nodes that have something to do with marital relations). Use sets for very rigorous handling of data (a set for documents not coded yet, a set for nodes without definitions...) Icon color can be used to differentiate further between documents in a set.

Use the Set Editor whenever you use sets! It is a tool for quick scanning and hunch-chasing, asking questions of, and rethinking sets, not only for making and reviewing them. If you are curious about a set of documents or nodes, play with the filter in the Set Editor to find what their attributes and coding look like.

◆ Use Trees to catalogue nodes. Use case nodes to keep track of data about cases by case type. Use a hierarchical node system as a taxonomy, a way of organizing, visualizing and locating items or categories, alerting you not only to where things easily "go" but also to areas that are muddy, unclear. A node system helps store things and helps find them again, (fast) and find related things easily, provides information about the body of knowledge it represents, and often prompts action. Like a library catalog it will tell you in moments what's not coming up. Like a recipe card box it reveals your data collection strategies (or those of your data collectors). Use the node system to show your project. Supervisors of research projects using the NUD*IST3 and 4 software, which pioneered hierarchical node systems in qualitative computing, find their students' node systems offer a very helpful picture of where a project has got to, and where it needs to go. Drop it into a model to show it live.

♦ Use Modeling for what sets and Trees do not do – showing and labelling and layering the *connections the researcher makes between* things. The Modeler is designed to show and store any visual representation of items. Don't wait to use it till you have something that deserves the title of Theory. It can be used as you use a whiteboard or a scratchpad, to scribble tentative ideas, try out different ways of organizing concepts, or produce a working guess of what is going on. It can also be used as a communication medium, to sketch a hypothesis, display rival interpretations or convey the different ideas of team members. Use it to try out ways of organizing nodes in trees, or plan possible next stage in the research design. on the basis of interpretation of the data.

Each of these ways of ordering and organizing is designed to be highly flexible, and the tools will be much more useful if they are flexed. Sets can be created, filtered, altered and deleted swiftly, without in any way damaging the data. They are designed to be created on the fly, to ask a question, scope a search or sort out the issues that matter for a particular task. Whenever you need to scoop some data together for a purpose, reach for a set. Think sets for any task that would be repetitive. For example, if you want to code a lot of documents entirely at one node (because they are all concerning a topic), create a new set, drag them all in, select this set in the Scope area of the Search tool and code the Scope at the required node. (And at any other nodes they all should be coded at.)

Trees too are highly flexible. Aim to build a system of nodes that elegantly represents the shape of your project. Use this picture of your ideas to monitor development of the project. The Set Editor and Search Tool both offer ways of interrogating the index system. (Which nodes don't have coding? How do these two overlap?) Now, within that shape, you can constantly refine and tidy the index system, using the quick processes of cut, copy, paste, merge.

The Modeler, too, is designed for flexibility. Use the ability to Save As, to keep different versions of a model as a history of your organizing and ordering of ideas. Use Layers and Groups to record growing and changing understandings. As the models build up, use the ability to jump from the model to the data represented by an icon, moving between the picture of how things are falling into place, and the data behind those "things".

Each of these ways of ordering and organizing is also a way of seeing and clarifying patterns. Neither the Modeler nor the Trees do what Sets do. In a useful hierarchical index, or in a model, an item occurs once. Since each node is part of your vocabulary of concepts, each node has a place. By contrast, a node or document can occur in many sets, since sets are not a taxonomy, but a way of bundling things to think about.

Pathways to analysis tools

The integration of tools in NVivo is complete in the sense that none of the choices above leaves you unable to go on to analysis processes. But they take your analysis in different directions. Of the options described, the visual ones – using rich text editing for visual coding, and using models for displaying theories and ideas – offer alternatives to other analysis processes. So visual coding offers a first way of marking up and shaping data. Modeling offers the chance to visualize ideas at any stage – and return to the data.

Each of the other tools described above – the document system and node system, document and node attributes, coding, sets and data links – is directly integrated with each of the analysis tools. The options for filtering sets, for example, in the Set Editor, include a wide range of questions you can ask about coding, attributes and other features. By filtering sets you can change the scope of a search. By scoping the search you can focus and refocus as you pursue ideas. By saving results of the search as a set you can ask more questions about coding, attributes and other features of those documents or nodes.

As you make choices about ways of developing categories, linking data and ideas, coding, bringing together and teasing apart data, ordering and organizing, informs those choices by checking what you can do next.

Viewing and pattern finding

What you do next may well be to ask a "Wh-" question; there are places in most processes for this new capability of NVivo. Profile documents or nodes to find which have coding or when they were modified, or whose they are in the team. Gather them in sets and use the filter in the Set Editor to pursue hunches (bet it's all the men who are saying this!). Assay the scope of a search before you do it (now that I have focused on divorced women, which cases are coming up?). Familiarity with the various filtering, profiling and searching options will allow you to keep asking, whenever you want a glimpse of the data, as well as to make searches, test hypotheses and profile reports from more formal inquiry.

There is considerable choice in the ways you see data and see the patterns in data in NVivo.

The Browsers showing the text of a document or the text coded at a node offer important choices. Note how differently you see that text in the different contexts, and what else you can do in and from each Browser. Check the range of ways of seeing text in the Node Browser, varying how much text you see for each passage coded there, and how much context you can view behind it for possible coding. Use either the Document or the Node

Browser with coding stripes displayed, and you will find you "see" the data differently again, colored (literally) by the coding results of your interpretation.

The four Explorers are for viewing and manipulating the documents, nodes, attributes or models therein. But even in these very directed tools there are choices. Apparently cosmetic advantages like colored icons and drag and drop making of sets are there to assist you in rapidly adapting how you see your project to what you want to do. In the Attribute Explorer, find out and use the options that allow you to order and select the items viewed.

From documents, nodes, (and sets of them) as well as attributes you have the option to create on the screen an immediate profile of the data. Profiles can show you a very wide range of information or coding about documents, nodes and attributes. Use profiles to ask what you have here, to display a suspected pattern, or just to keep tabs on the data collection process – and of course to export to table software. Use the special table, produced by a Matrix search in the Search Tool, for displays with visual impact – you can see from the shading of the cells where the pattern is falling. Now do some real qualitative work on that suspected pattern: click on any cell to browse the contents, spread context, jump to source. This is an impressive conference display tool!

Getting it together with statistical data

There are many reasons qualitative researchers wish to link with data in statistical packages or spreadsheets. Linking of qualitative and quantitative data with sophisticated software does much more than simply juxtapose two different sorts of data. NVivo is designed to handle and use subtly in qualitative processes the information about attributes or coding that is properly often stored in quantitative form. So it is also designed to make movement of such information two-way and efficient. You can import attribute values and export attribute values or coding, or any other information about documents or nodes that can be presented in profiles.

How to do this is described in the Reference Manual (Chapter 11 on Reports and Profiles, Chapter 12 on Importing and Exporting and Appendix A on file formats). NVivo's online Help files also contain detailed instructions. This section is intended to give you a summary overview of why you might be doing this, and how to choose between the ways to make those connections.

Import attributes

Data that is in a statistical package (or any other table-based software) can be imported into NVivo as Attributes. Tables are simple to prepare in any table-based software; using the option to save as tab-separated text you create the table immediately in the form NVivo imports. Note the table will import values of existing attributes of any type, or create attributes of one specified value type. If you have data to import with many value types, either set the attributes up first in NVivo, or make separate tables for different value types.

This import process will create the nodes or documents specified in the table if they do not exist. This means it is another way of creating new nodes or new, empty editable documents. You can set up your NVivo project this way with the entry of preparatory data (perhaps from a first questionnaire stage of your in-depth interview project). *See Chapter 5 of this book and the Reference Manual for details about attributes and values.*

Export attributes

You may have created or changed the attributes of documents or nodes in the NVivo project, and wish to export them to a statistics package, spreadsheet etc. Or your qualitative analysis in NVivo may have resulted in a shaping of data that is well expressed in attributes (for example a typology). Simply make a report of the selected attributes for selected documents or nodes.

Exporting coding (and a lot of other information!)

There are many ways to do this, and the choice depends on your goals. You can export table-based software to any Profile of a document or document set, node or node set. Profile tables can contain information about coding, data management etc. *(see Chapter 3).* The Assay tool in Search provides a particularly useful export form, since the cells contain whether or not the scope items are coded at particular nodes or have particular attribute values. You can also export a Matrix created in the search tool. You might, for example, create a matrix of case nodes by attitudes to authority, explore that qualitatively, using the ability to browse the text for each cell, then once satisfied, export to the statistics package in which you are examining these cases quantitatively. From any of these tables in NVivo you can create a table that statistics packages and spreadsheets can read.

Design Issues

But before you do it, what is it you want to do? This is another area where NVivo offers a range of functions, and methodologically informed choice is necessary. Importing or exporting bulk variable-type data can be overwhelming to a researcher whose goals are unclear. Explore first the processes and options.

There are strong capabilities for arranging, selecting and editing items in all table-based software and in NVivo's table-based attribute and coding profiles. These will support selecting exactly what you know you want to use in qualitative inquiry from the possibly very large numbers of variables in your statistics package. The best advice is to import only the variables you know you will use, and later import others if they prove important.

Before you export from NVivo, exercise the same selective caution. As you get familiar with the import-export facilities, you will find it easy to do quick data transfers for focused purposes and to present data in ways that immediately make it accessible for qualitative work. To take a simple example, if you import document attributes for a large survey before creating the documents that will contain the open-ended questions, there will be a lot of documents to delete! But the ability to create documents by importing attributes might be an extraordinary benefit to a researcher bringing into NVivo the fieldwork component of a hitherto quantitative project. Each actor in the situation you are studying has a new, rich text document created, ready for your field notes.

Getting it together from the start

This final section is for the many qualitative researchers who always experience the beginning of a project as an explosion of unpredictable experience, data, confusion. In the design of NVivo, we set out to assist researchers in starting immediately, without preempting data, or discoveries from it. The ability to combine rich text editing and writing of documents with coding and linking, in integrated processes, allows you to avoid delaying reflection till coding is done, and explore data as it accrues. This means too that the researcher is far more able to account for the research process, document what is happening and critique it as it happens.

If this is your aim, you will find that the editable compound documents in NVivo give a unique opportunity to hold your project together, revisit and assess it and not lose related material. A good way to start a project, and a good way to play with NVivo's toolkit, is to begin by making a first document in NVivo's editor and have it grow as the project grows.

Audit document

In some fields (educational evaluation and epidemiology, for example) auditing of research processes is frequently required. In most it is advisable. The researcher must account for each stage in the research process, including research design, sample construction and access, data handling and coding procedures, ways of questioning, searching and validating theories. Without such audits, the fluidity and complexity of qualitative data can be problematic especially to researchers used to numerical data and unused to the cumulative nature of qualitative theory construction.

A compound document provides the medium to maintain just the required record of research process and procedure. Since the document can contain DataLinks to other documents or nodes, it need not become onerous to maintain or store. To begin, simply create a new document in NVivo's editor, and start typing in rich text. Note you can date any entry by selecting Insert Date and Time from the Edit menu.

Copy or type in notes on major research stages and link them to other files or documents in or out of the project. Lists of the nodes in your index system at a particular stage can be linked, to tell the story of your growing conceptual scheme. Literature summaries provide background to your inquiry or justify decisions. Spreadsheets of sample characteristics at different stages, account for theoretical sampling. Early memos about new concepts, or papers written about the first stages of analysis; layered NVivo models of the different stages in theory construction.

At each stage of analysis, you can record the detail NVivo provides on the outcomes of analysis, including the results of assaying and scoping searches. (Make DataBites to assay tables reporting what has been found; a DocLink takes the reader to the Memo about this line of inquiry.)

This plum-pudding-like document can be edited at any stage to make an impressive and thorough account of the data. When an audit is required, save it in rich text, and produce it in a word processor with the illustrations and tables, and any quotations from linked data, presented within the full account of the project history.

Project Document

Qualitative researchers need always to be able to see the project as a whole and hold onto the developing aspects of it. Try starting with a Project Document which grows and links to other parts of the project. This could be less formal (and much less tidy!) than an audit document. The tutorials show several variants of this approach. In "Get on With Living", for example, the project starts with a design document linked to background material and research proposals, information about the researcher and goals. As the project grows, the document grows with it. It may become your private research diary, your way of keeping in touch with your supervisor or the draft of your methods chapter.

Use it as you used to use notebooks with diary entries. It might start as a brief outline of the research issues and puzzles, growing as it records the first design. Create a new document in NVivo's editor, (or import the word processor document that contains your grant application, thesis proposal or excited letter to a colleague about the research opportunity) and start typing in rich text. This beginning may suit a qualitative project better than building up a heap of documents containing the "original" data, and then commencing analysis, a sequence more appropriate to survey research. The Project Document grows as you learn more, creating more documents that record research experience.

It will undoubtedly become a more compound document, with DataLinks to personal memoirs, photos, discoveries in the literature (or library search results identifying reading to be done), your despairing voice late at night, the tape of a video conference and the presentation of the prize at the end of the project! Other DataLinks take you to everything about sampling in early proposals, or the particular place in a grant proposal where you addressed a methods issue or memos about a core category that failed. In the text insert DataBites (annotations about problems yet to be faced; a diagram of the project stages; your supervisor's encouraging voice!). Keep these documents in their own sets: some hold the material from your literature review, some transcripts of pilot interviews, and the Search tool allows you to select which question you go to.

And now, viewing, teaching, presenting

Qualitative computing brought three new challenges for researchers who need to show and share their data and analysis processes. Once the project is "in" a package, it is inaccessible to those without the software.

The first challenge is making an ongoing project accessible to those who should monitor and advise. How to allow review or critiquing of analysis by the supervisor who doesn't know the software, or the client or research collaborator who is not a qualitative researcher?

The second challenge is for teachers who wish to use their own data in teaching software. How to involve students or workshop participants in data relevant to them if they have only free demonstration software with "canned" tutorials?

And thirdly, the challenging task of rich presentation of rich projects. How to show to the team or the conference all the data that justify the report?

QSR responded with a free no-save version of NVivo that can be given to colleagues to view a project, and used for teaching purposes to run, in no-save mode, any data provided.

Free project viewer

Anyone can view a project within NVivo. The Viewer is available free. It allows full access to the project data, with all the tools of NVivo except the ability to save changes.

Give the free Viewer, with your project, to your supervisor; your client in a commissioned project or team in an action research project. NVivo is easy to access, and viewing does not require detailed training in the software. To guide their viewing, write a project document outlining issues, and containing DataLinks to memo documents, or to nodes coding data to be discussed. Create a model of current analysis, and show the viewing colleague how to click on each item to read it. Since NVivo allows copying and pasting of text into another application, they can write commentary, discuss particular passages etc. in a word processor or an email message – but not alter the project.

Make your own tutorial

NVivo comes, either in the full or demonstration version, with five tutorials, two offering two stages, offering different approaches to setting up a project, with different sorts of data. But teachers and trainers often wish to provide data relevant to a class. And self-teaching researchers may wish to practise on their own data, asking questions that really matter to them.

For those who want to learn or teach with their own data, the tutorial mode, on either the free demonstration software or full software, will support placing your own project to be run in no-save mode.

Computer presentations

Presenting qualitative research persuasively is always a challenge. With so much rich data backing every conclusion, and so many threads to every theme, the researcher may be left convinced the data has been misrepresented, or only thinly seen by the audience or reviewer.

Many aspects of NVivo assist presentations of projects. Either the full software or the Viewer can display compound documents with DataLinks. Click on the link to move swiftly from the description of data to the image or voice, to detailed illustrations, or all the quotations supporting them. Either the full software or the Viewer can display layered models that show how your theory was developed and are linked directly to the data they represent.

Getting help

NVivo is designed, developed and documented from within a team that works with qualitative researchers, teaching software and learning from teaching it, from discussion lists about it and methodological debates. The results of this work are not only software packages but contributions to academic conferences and publications. References are on the website. The team at QSR seeks feedback, debate and always new directions: contact us through help@qsr.com.au.

QSR also works with colleagues who wish to help and train other researchers using the software, provide materials for teaching it and help in using it. If you want a workshop or some advice it is probably available from someone near you or someone you can email. Help sources are detailed on the QSR website. If you want to become a trainer, or find yourself helping other researchers, contact help@qsr.com.au for assistance.

Internet Resources

The QSR software web site www.qsr.com.au contains technical support tips, demonstration software and utilities for converting early version databases. You can also find references, training materials and other documents. Software registration can be performed on-line.

QSR operates mirror sites www.qsr-software.com and www.qsr-software.co.uk in North America and England.

Discussion Forum

If you want a debate or a discussion it is easily created on the QSR-Forum. If you wish to join an ongoing email forum of NUD*IST users and qualitative researchers, follow the instructions below. Email a request to mailing-list-request@qsr.com.au with the following contained in the body of the message: **SUBSCRIBE qsr-forum yourfirstname yourlastname**. Instructions to leave the forum are included on every forum message.

Glossary

Access

See Project Access

Administrator

See Project Administrator.

Alias

When a Document or Node is placed in a Set, it is not copied to there; instead if you access it from the Set you are taken to the actual item, which resides in the Document or Node System respectively. Its representation in the Set is called an Alias or Shortcut, and removing the Alias from the Set does not delete the Document or Node it points to.

Anchor

An icon in a Document which connects to other Documents 📄 or Nodes 🌳; or a green underlined passage connecting to a DataBite.

Analysis

The process of exploring a Project's data to discover or build or test relationships and patterns; primarily using the Search Tool or the graphical Modeler, but also the Sets Editor, Attribute Explorer and Assay Tool

Annotation

A short text passage that the user writes, usually to comment on a passage in a Document, and linked to it as a DataBite.

Assay

A fast analysis process in which various properties of a Set or a Search Scope can be explored, such as checking which members of the set are coded by a selected Node.

Assay Tool

A control available in the Search Tool, for doing Assays.

Attribute

An Attribute is a named generic property the user can give to all Nodes, or to all Documents; e.g. 'Age', 'Marital Status'. Each Document or Node is given a specific Value for the Attribute, e.g. '49', 'single'. Values can be of type Boolean, Date-Time, Numeric, or String . NVivo also supplies three different "null" values.

Attribute Editor

A window for creating and altering attributes (their names and descriptions), and defining the values an attribute can take.

Attribute Explorer

A window showing a table of selected attributes and documents or nodes, with the body of the table showing the values of each attribute for each document or node. Provides controls for altering values, plus other facilities.

Attribute Lookup

A type of Search. Finds the passages in the scope items that belong to documents with a selected Attribute Value, or are coded by nodes with the selected Attribute Value.

Attribute Value

See Attribute

Boolean Search

A class of Searches. Finds passages in the Scope Items that have a particular boolean combination of features. Combinations are Intersection (and), Union (or), Difference (less), Negation (not), Matrix Intersection and Matrix Difference.

Browser

Window showing the contents of one Project item, e.g. a Document or a Node. Browsers have controls for manipulating the item.

Case

An particular instance of a general type of thing, e.g. a particular patient history. In NVivo these are conveniently handled as Case Nodes.

Case Node

A Case Node is intended to represent an instance of a particular type of thing, – e.g. a patient history. Case Nodes of the same type, e.g. the patient histories, are grouped as children of one Case Type Node, e.g. 'Patient History'.

Case Node Area

The subsystem of the Node system that holds Case Type and Case Nodes.

Case Node Title

Every Case and Case Type Node has a "specific" Title which must be different from its siblings. Its syntax rules are as for Free Node Titles. A given Case or Case Type Node can then be identified by its "hierarchical" Title, formed by stringing together the specific Titles of all the Nodes in the path from the top ("root") of the Case Node System, down to the given Node, and with periods in front of each Case Type Node, and a colon in front of the Case Node, e.g. '.Members.Patients:Anton'.

Case Sensitive

If two words or strings are recognized as different even though they only differ over the case of some letters, e.g. 'MacKay' and 'Mackay', then the recognition is said to be Case Sensitive.

Case Type Node

In the Case Area, all cases of a given type, e.g. all the employees (as nodes 'Smith', 'Schmidt', etc.) are grouped as children of a Case Type Node representing their common type, here 'Employee'.

Children Nodes

In the Tree Node and Case Node Systems, all the Nodes directly linked to the selected Node from below.

Clipboard

See NVivo Clipboard

Code [verb]

The action of assigning passages of text from a Document to a Node. The Node is then said to code that passage of the document.

See Coding Passage.

Coders

Tools used to Code a Document, or to Code-On at a Node. Particularly, the Coder boxes associated with Document and Node Browsers.

Coding

See Coding Passage

Coding Context

The text surrounding a Coding Passage in a Document. Users can view the Passage in a selected context, and can spread (extend the Coded Passage) to the context., such as surrounding Paragraph or Section.

Coding-On

Process of reviewing and re-coding the passages from earlier coding at a node, typically using the Node Browser. Used to refine coding, to create finer categories, and to distinguish dimensions of a concept.

Coding Passage

Nodes in a Project can contain references to text from Documents in the Project. The text corresponding to such a reference is called a Coding Passage, and collectively are called the Node's Coding. A node is said to contain references to, or code, several Passages from several Documents.

Coding Stripes

Vertical lines in the right-hand pane of a Document or Node Browser, showing approximately where selected Nodes Code the displayed text. The exact Passages can be highlighted by use of the Coder.

Control Pads

The Launch Pad (when NVivo is in Overview Mode) and the Project Pad (when in Project Mode). Provide access to all available processes. Closing a Control Pad shuts down NVivo.

Co-occurrence Search (near)

A type of Proximity Search. Finds passages in the Scope Items having one particular feature and passages having a second particular feature, that are near to each other. Nearness can be overlapping, in the same paragraph, in the same Scope Document or Section of a stated level, and in the same coded passage of a Scope Node.

Copy

Data from one place in a Project database can often be placed somewhere else, e.g. a text passage from a Document, together with its coding. This is called 'copying' if the new item is a duplicate of the old. Contrast 'Alias'.

DAT file

A plain text file containing data for a table in Tab-Separated Format, in a form suitable for importation into SPSS; also as exported from SPSS.

Database

See Project Database

DataBite, DataBite Link

A small piece of text written by the user (Annotation) or an external computer file, that the user links to a piece of text in a Document. The anchor text is green and underlined. On selecting the anchor, the linked DataBite can be displayed.

DataLink

Any of three types of links can be made from a Document or Node to other data. They are: DocLinks 📄, NodeLinks 🔧, and green underlined DataBite Links. See also Memo, Extract.

Default Value

The value for a particular item that NVivo uses if it has to have one but the user hasn't specified it, for example, the Title of a newly created Node.

Difference Search

A type of Boolean Search. It finds passages in the Scope Items having any of one collection of features but not any of a second collection.

DocLink

A DataLink, linking a Document or Node to a Document. Can be a link from the Document or Node as a whole ("Top-level Link"), or anchored anywhere in a Document's text (with the icon 📄) to make a link from that point in the text. See Memo.

Document

A Document in an NVivo Project is an editable file of rich text together with a range of Document Properties it has. The Document may be coded by Nodes, may be given Values of Document Attributes, may contain DataLinks for direct access to related Documents, Nodes, Annotations, and External Computer Files.

Document Description

The user can attach to any Document a brief description, usually of the origin, type, etc. of the Document.

Document Icon

A distinctively shaped icon to represent Documents. The user can choose its color.

Document Length

The number of characters in a Document's text, not including DocLink or NodeLink icons.

Document Explorer

A window listing all of a Project's Documents and Document Sets, with tools for handling those Documents.

Document Name

Documents in a Project are identified by their Names. A Name can be changed, and must be at most 36 characters long, preferably under 12. No two Documents can have the same Name, and Names are not case sensitive.

Document Property

A feature of any Project Document that is recorded by NVivo, and may be used for information or to help frame analyses etc. They are: Name, Description, Creation date & time, Modification Date & Time, Owner, is Memo?, Icon color, Document's origin.

Document Section

Parts of Documents, of different Levels, marked by a Heading at their beginning, and stopping at the next Heading of higher Level or at the end of the Document - in other words lower level Sections are nested in higher Level ones. There are nine levels of Sections, 1 is highest. A Document as a whole, especially text before the first Heading, is sometimes regarded as at Level 0.

Document Source

A computer file, non-computer document or other source of information, from which the contents of a particular Project Document are obtained.

Document System

The part of an NVivo Project's database in which all the Project's Documents are kept.

Explorer

A window showing all the Project's database items of the same type, e.g. the Document Explorer.

Export

The process of outputting data files from a Project in a form that can be read by other programs, such as a word processor or spreadsheet program.

External File

A computer file referred to in a Project's database but that is not an actual part of the database; e.g. a Project Document is often copied from a file somewhere on the computer system, and a reference to that file is kept for the user's information.

Extract Node

Where one Document refers to something recorded in another one, the user can insert a NodeLink at that point in the first Document, linked to the relevant text in the second one, but extracted from it as a new Node. Such a Node can be flagged as an Extract, to indicate its purpose. Extracts are like ordinary footnote citations, only they show the cited text. They are like coding in reverse.

Free Node, Free Node Area

A Node that has not been classified as a Tree, Case or Case Type Node, kept in the Free Node Area. Free Nodes are useful for storing concepts and coding that is yet to be organized into a useful place in the Node System for future access, like uncatalogued books in a library.

Free Node Title

The Node Title for a Free Node. Syntax rules: at most 36 characters (12 or under is recommended), and may contain spaces. It must not contain "/" (slash), ":" (colon), "." (period), or "(" or ")" (parentheses). It may contain digits but it must not be only digits.

Given Value of an Attribute

A "significant" value of the attribute, assigned by the user to the document or node. Opposed to a Null Value.

Graphical Model

See Model.

Group

A way of associating items in a Model, typically used for functionally related items. Items in a Group can be displayed as enhanced compared to other items. Groups extend across all models in a project, to enable comparative work where different models capture related scenarios. Compare Layer.

Guest Access

A mode of access to a Project for someone who is not a Project Team Member. The user must log in to the Project with the name 'Guest' and a password provided by the Project's Administrator.

Icon

A graphic symbol associated with types of items in a Project such as Documents and Nodes; or symbolizing some action such as opening a DataBite.

Importation

The process of bringing into a Project, data from a file that belongs to some other program. Project Documents can be created by importing RTF files made in a word processor, and Attribute data can be imported from a spreadsheet file.

Inclusion Search (surrounding)

A type of Proximity Search. Finds passages in the Scope Items having one particular feature that surround passages having a second particular feature.

Intersection Search (and)

A type of Boolean Search. It finds passages in the Scope Items having all of a given collection of features (this *and* that *and* the next feature).

In Vivo coding

A code, or the process of coding, in which a text selection in a Document becomes the title of the Node that codes that text.

Item

See Model Item

Item Link

In a Model, the lines, sometimes arrowed and labeled, that can join two items together. Links like Model Items can represent a Document, Node, Attribute, Set, another Model, or any entity the user chooses – where these are seen as relational in nature.

Label

In the Modeler, the name given to and displayed on an Item or Link. Not necessarily the same as the name of the Document etc. the Item or Link may *represent*. E.g. a crime scene model may have a "Murderer" item which represents the "Rev. Green" Node but in an exploratory scenario change you make it represent the "Miss Scarlett" node.

Launch Pad

NVivo's Control Pad window when in Overview Mode, providing access to all Overview processes and opening or creating Projects.

Layer

A way of associating items in a Model, typically used for handling categorization. Items in a layer can be displayed independently of other items in the Model. Layers extend across all models in a project, to enable comparative work where different models capture related scenarios. Compare Group.

Level

See Document Section.

Link

An overworked term.

1. Links from Documents and Nodes to other items – see DataLink, DocLink, NodeLink, DataBite.

2. Lines drawn in a Model – see Item Link

3. The connection between a Node and its parent or children in the Node System – see Tree Node.

Matrix, Matrix Search

A Matrix is the result of a type of search in which a search operator is mapped across two collections of input Nodes, Attribute Values and/ or Text Search Patterns. The operator is applied to each pair of items made by taking one item from the first collection and one from the second collection, producing a table of results.

Matrix Co-occurrence

A type of Proximity Search. It carries out a Co-occurrence Search using two collections of features. Taking one feature from each collection at a time, it finds passages in the Scope Items having the feature from the first collection, and passages having the second feature, that are near to each other. It then makes a table of all the results.

Matrix Difference

A type of Boolean Search. It carries out a Difference Search using two collections of features. Taking one feature from each collection at a time, it finds passages in the Scope Items having the feature from the first collection but not the second; and makes a table of all the results.

Matrix Inclusion

A type of Proximity Search. It carries out an Inclusion Search using two collections of features. Taking one feature from each collection at a time, it finds passages in the Scope Items having the feature from the first collection, that surround passages having the second feature. It then makes a table of all the results.

Matrix Inspector

A window displaying the results of a Matrix Search as an interactive table with a range of controls.

Matrix Intersection

A type of Boolean Search. It carries out an Intersection Search using two collections of features. Taking one feature from each collection at a time, it finds passages in the Scope Items having both features; and makes a table of all the results.

Matrix Node

When a Matrix search completes, the cells of the table are stored as sibling Nodes, called Matrix Nodes, in the Tree Node System under a so-called Matrix Parent Node which describes how the search was done.

Matrix Parent Node

The parent of a Matrix Node in the Tree Node Area.

Matrix Profile

See Matrix Inspector

Matrix Sequence

A type of Proximity Search. It carries out a Sequence Search using two collections of features. Taking one feature from each collection at a time, it finds passages in the Scope Items having the feature from the first collection, and passages having the second feature, that are near to each other, but with the first passage starting before the second one. It then makes a table of all the results.

Memo

A Project Document that the user regards as providing commentary, usually on a Node or another Document. Any Document can be flagged as a Memo, to assist in identifying ones with this purpose.

Model Explorer, Modeler

An Explorer window providing access to all Models. It can also display any one Model in its main pane, with controls for changing it.

Model, Modeling

A model is a diagram in which various objects, called Items, are connected by lines and arrows, called Links. Modeling in NVivo is quite sophisticated, with facilities for changing appearance, using layers and grouping, and making model items and links represent (and open onto) most types of entities in a project, such as documents, attributes, and other models.

Model Item

Any object that appears in a Model, representing a Document, Node, Attribute, Set, another Model, or any entity the user chooses. They can be joined by lines called Links, and assigned to Layers and Groups.

Most Recently Used Set

See Recently Used Set

Names

Used to identify Documents, Attributes, and Sets. Syntax rules: 36 characters maximum (12 or under is recommended), may contain spaces.

Negation Search

A type of Boolean Search. It finds all passages in the Scope Items having none of a given collection of features.

Node

An object in a Project which is intended to represent anything that Project users may wish to refer to, such as people being studied, concepts, places, mental states, features of the research as a Project. Nodes can be given Values of Attributes according to the features of what they represent, they can be grouped in Sets, and they can Code relevant passages in the Project's Documents. Nodes are stored in the Node System.

Node Area

All nodes in the Node System get stored in three different areas.
See Free Node Area, Tree Node Area, Case Node Area.

Node Description

The user can attach to any Node a brief Description, usually of the origin, purpose, meaning etc. of the Node. NVivo will provide Descriptions for Nodes that were created by a Search process, to record how they were made.

Node Explorer

A window listing all of a Project's Nodes and Node Sets, with tools for handling those Nodes.

NodeLink

A DataLink, linking a Document or Node to a Node. Can be a link from the Document or Node as a whole ("Top-level Link"), or anchored anywhere in a Document's text (with the icon 🔔) to make a link from that point in the text.
See Extract.

Node Lookup

A type of Search. Finds where a particular Node codes the Scope Items.

Node Property

A feature of any Project Node that is recorded by NVivo, and may be used for information or to help frame analyses etc. They are: Name, Description, Creation date & time, Modification Date & Time, Owner, is Extract?, and position in the Node System.

Node Subsystem

See Node Area

Node System

The part of an NVivo's Project database in which all the Nodes are kept. It is divided into Free Nodes, Tree Nodes and Case Nodes areas or systems.

Node Title

Nodes are identified by their Titles, which act as names. A Title can be changed. Titles are not case sensitive. Because of the hierarchical nature of parts of the Node System, Titles can be compound. See Free Node Title, Tree Node Title, Case Node Title.

Node Tree

See Tree Node System

Node Type

Types of Nodes are Free Node, Tree Node, Matrix Node and Matrix Parent Node, Case Node, and Case Type Node. These have different behaviors and uses, and occur in different Areas or Subsystems the Node System.

No-save Mode

A mode of running a project in which changes to the project's database do not get saved.

Null Value of an Attribute

A way of saying that a particular document or Node does not have a value for the attribute. The three null values are Not Assigned (-), Unknown (?) and Not Applicable (NA).

NVivo Clipboard

A smart version of the familiar clipboard used for carrying cut or copied items. In NVivo it can carry Nodes, Documents, passages from Documents together with their coding, and other items; and when pasting can work out what it is appropriate to paste.

Operator

See Search Operator

Overview Level

When a user is running NVivo, but does not have a Project open, NVivo is said to be in Overview Level, as opposed to Project Level. In Overview Level the user can use non-project aspects of NVivo, such as opening a Project, or editing a file.

Owner

The person who created a Node or Document is called its Owner. Ownership can be changed later, and is a useful property for analyzing progress in a Project.

Paragraph

In a Project Document, a paragraph is represented as a string of text beginning at the start of the file or just after a Carriage Return/Line Feed (CRLF) token, and terminates with the next CRLF token inclusive, or end-of-file.

Paragraph Coder

A coding window in which the user can code a Document in paragraph chunks, by referring to the ordinal number of the paragraphs in the Document (paragraph 1, 2, 3, etc.).

Paragraph Style

Paragraphs in a Document can be given a pre-set style such as 'Normal', 'Plain Text', 'Title'. Styles 'Heading 1' to 'Heading 9' are used to mark the start of Sections of that level.

Parent Node

In the Tree Node or Case-Node Systems, the Node directly linked to the selected Node from above.

Passage

See Coding Passage

Pattern

See Text Search Pattern

Plain Text File

A computer file containing just undecorated text, no special fonts, no character or paragraph styling. Plain text files can be imported into an NVivo Project as Documents. Can have various extensions, commonly TXT.

Profile, Profiling

A Profile is a table of Project data that can be displayed internally in the Project, and/or printed or exported for handling in table programs such as spreadsheets. Preparing and exploring the table is called Profiling.

Project

Like a research project. Users interact with NVivo by working in an NVivo Project. Each Project has a unitary collection of information that NVivo, and the user, handle as a whole. A user can work on only one NVivo Project at a time.

Project Access

A Project Administrator can set up a Project so that only certain types of access are available, e.g. by password for team members, read-only for guests, and not at all for others.

Project Administrator

The user who created the Project. The Administrator has "super-user" type powers to control setting up team members and access permissions, etc.

Project Database

The information about an NVivo Project that is stored persistently, i.e. from one run of the Project to the next.

Project Level

When a user has a Project open in NVivo, NVivo is said to be in Project Level, as opposed to Overview Level.

Project Pad

NVivo's Control Pad window when in Project Mode, providing access to all Project processes and main Project windows. May be "rolled up" from its Windows menu, but not closed.

Project Team

A Project Team comprises the users who are registered in a Project as permitted to access the Project and modify its data. Membership is controlled by the Project Administrator.

Properties Box

A window for displaying and modifying (where permitted) the properties of a Document or Node, such as its Description and Creation Date; or of the Project.

Proximity Search

A class of Searches. Finds passages in the Scope Items with one particular feature that are close in some way to passages with a second particular feature. Particular Proximity Searches are Co-occurrence (near), Sequence (preceding), Inclusion (surrounding), Matrix Co-occurrence, and Matrix Inclusion.

Proxy Document

A project Document a user can create to represent source data. It is used primarily to hold summaries or commentaries on the Source, and sometimes DataBites linked to fragments of the Source if it's on-line, e..g. a video file.

Recently Used Document

A Document in the Set of Recently Used Documents.

Recently Used Node

A Node in the Set of Recently Used Nodes.

Recently Used Set

Two Sets, holding the ten Documents and Nodes that have been most recently modified in some way, e.g. Documents that have been edited or coded. The user may not edit these Sets.

Report

A Rich Text Format file the user can create as output from a Project, to record many different types of Project data.

Representation

In the Modeler, an Item or Link can be associated with a Document, Node, Attribute, Attribute Value, Set, or other Model; then from the item or link you can access the represented entity.

Retrieval

A Coding Passage in a Document that has been retrieved from the Project Database to display in some way.

Rich Text File

Any file in Rich Text Format (.RTF extension) that can be handled fully by NVivo. These files can have various fonts, character styles, paragraph styles, etc., unlike Plain Text Files.

Root Node

In the Tree Node and Case-Node Systems, a Node that has no Parent Node in the Tree, hence is the "root" of the Tree.

Scope, Scope Item

A Scope is the Project data that the user chooses for a particular search operation to work on. It consists of a selection of Documents and/or Nodes, called the Scope Items.

Search, Search Operation

An Analysis operation involving the exploration of a Scope of Documents and/or Nodes, to find various features defined by a Search Operation using the scope items' coding, attribute values and/or text.

Search Operator, Search Operand

A Search Operation always contains an action specification called its Operator, such as 'Find matches to this text pattern….' or 'Find text passages coded by … and ….' The items the Operator acts on (filling these dots) are its Operands or Arguments, e.g. a text pattern (for the text search Operator above) or two Nodes (for the Intersection Operator above).

Search Results

Various ways of collecting the finds made in a search operation, often as one or more Nodes.

Search Scope
See Scope

Search Tool
A window for controlling the setting up and running of a Search.

Section
See Document Section

Sequence Search (preceding)
A type of Proximity Search. Finds passages in the Scope Items having one particular feature and passages having a second particular feature, that are near to each other, but with the first passage starting before the second one. Nearness can be overlapping, in the same paragraph, in the same Scope Document or Section of a stated level, and in the same coded passage of a Scope Node.

Set
A named collection of Documents or of Nodes that NVivo handles as a unity. Actual Documents and Nodes are not stored in Sets, instead the Set's members are Aliases (shortcuts or pointers) to the actual Document or Node stored in the Document or Node System. A given Document or Node can be a member of any number of Sets.

Shortcut
See Alias

Sibling Nodes
In the Tree Node and Case Node Areas, Nodes with the same Parent Node.

Source
See Document Source

Special Character
Text characters that need to be written in a Text Search Pattern in a special way, e.g. using "\p" to match the end-of-paragraph character. They are marked by a backslash then a character.

Spread [of coding]
Any Coding Passage can be automatically widened to include some surrounding text – a process called Spreading. Available options are to the enclosing paragraph(s) or section, or even document.

Standard Node Order
The order in which nodes are shown in the Node Explorer's left pane:

1. Free Nodes, lexically on their titles
2. Tree Nodes, numerical order of addresses
3. Case Type/Case nodes, lexically on full titles.

String
Any sequence of characters of text, whether or not they make words or grammatical sense.

Style (Modeler)
In the Modeler, an Item or Link can be given a Style, which is a named collection of visible properties, such as its color, the font for its label, its size or thickness, etc.

Style Marker
A code or markup that is put at the beginning of a paragraph in a Plain Text File to determine its Rich Text style when imported as a Project Document.

Sub tree
In the Tree Node or Case Node Systems, the Tree formed by taking a particular Node (often called the Root of the Sub-tree) and all its descendants – the nodes that can be reached from it by links going downwards.

System Closure
Analyses, retrievals etc. done in an NVivo project can be kept in the project as subject material awaiting further analysis, typically as Nodes. Systems whose results are subject material are called "closed", e.g. history where you study writings of historians as much as "primary" texts, and tend to deny any hard conceptual distinction between the two.

Tab-separated file format
A type of plain text file for exporting and importing data tables. The fields in each record (row) are separated by tabs, and the rows are separated by carriage return-line feed tokens.

Team
A Team for a Project is the group of people whom the Project recognizes as permitted to work on the Project.

Text File
See Plain Text File, Rich Text File

Text Search
A type of Search. Finds strings of text in Documents, or passages coded by a Node, that match a Text Search Pattern.

Text Search Pattern
Specification of the text to be located in a text search. A pattern can be simple – just the string to be matched, e.g. "Mary", or contain Wildcards and Special Characters.

Title

See Node Title

Tree

Describes the branching structure of the Tree Node System and Case-Node System.

Tree Node, Tree Node Area

Nodes in the Tree Node System are organized in a so-called Tree structure. Here, a Node is linked to one "parent" Node above it – more generic in nature – and to any number of more specific "children" Nodes below it. Like library catalogues or taxonomies, which are tree-structured, the purpose of the Tree Node System is to catalogue Nodes by grouping similar ones as "siblings" under a generic parent, enabling fast location of a Node by its meaning, content or purpose, rather than by its name.

Tree Node Address

To identify Tree Nodes, the user gives them each a number, 1 or greater, which must be different from its siblings. A Tree Node can then be identified by its Address, the series of Tree Node Numbers from the top ("root") of the Tree Node System down to the Node. Example: the Address '(4 6 2)' means, "start at top-level Node 4, find its child 6, and find child 2 of that." Node Numbers can be changed if they do not cause a clash with the number of a sibling Node.

Tree Node Area

The part of the Node System that contains Tree Nodes, Matrix Parent and Matrix Nodes. These nodes are linked upwards to a single Parent node, and downwards to any number of Children Nodes (mutually called Siblings).

Tree Node Number

See Tree Node Address

Tree Node Title

Every Tree Node has a "specific" Title which must be different from its siblings. Its syntax rules are as for Free Node Titles. A given Tree Node can then be identified by its "hierarchical" Title, formed by stringing together the specific Titles of all the Nodes in the path from the top ("root") of the Tree Node System, down to the given Node, and with slashes in front of each, e.g. '/Events/Accidents/Rear Ender'.

Tutorial

An NVivo project that is prepared for teaching purposes by adding explanatory text to guide the user. It is placed in a special Tutorials folder, intended to be opened using Overview Level tutorial access controls.

Tutorial Mode

A way of running a tutorial project when it is accessed directly from NVivo's tutorial access controls at Overview Level – which puts restrictions on saving and other aspects. By opening such a project in the normal way, tutorial mode is avoided.

TXT file extension

Extension commonly used for a Plain Text File. Plain text files with special layout features can have other extensions, such as DAT for use in the SPSS statistics package.

Union Search (or)

A type of Boolean Search. It finds all passages in the Scope Items having any of a given collection of features (this *or* that *or* the next feature)

Value

See Attribute Value

Viewer Version

A version of NVivo that will not save changes to project databases. Available freely as a demonstration version, and as a viewer for studying NVivo projects.

Visual Coding

The practice of emphasizing passages of text by using rich text features, as a visual counterpart of coding at nodes.

Wildcard

In a text search pattern, a component that in effect commands a special matching process at that point in the pattern. E.g. in the pattern "c.t", the wildcard "." means 'match any single character', so the pattern will match "cat" and "cot" but not "ct" or "coot".

Working Set

A semi-automatically maintained Set of Documents or Nodes that the user is currently working on, particularly in the Coder. It is provided solely for user convenience.

Index